"This is a brilliant, inspiring book that teaches and guides teens to navigate their inner world, as well as the world they live in. In a masterful piece, Schab has encompassed all aspects of teenagers' experience: body, mind, spirit, and relationships. The workbook format offers results-oriented lessons for a lifetime of healthy self-esteem. I highly recommend this book to anyone who has a teenager or has ever been one."

> —**Susan Schwass, LCSW**, private practitioner working with teens and their families for thirty-five years

"*The Self-Esteem Workbook for Teens* actively engages students in a gentle self-exploration of the ways both internal and external factors influence their self-perceptions and wellbeing. The workbook is set up with a logical flow that provides information, engages the student in thoughtful self-analysis, and offers reflection on one's individual strengths and positive attributes. Additionally, the workbook guides students in changing behaviors and thought processes detrimental to their wellbeing. The scenarios in the book provide relatable, real-life situations of which the adolescent can easily make sense."

> —**Wendy Merryman, PhD**, counselor in the Central Dauphin School District, working to promote positive personal, social, emotional, and academic growth of students in individual, small-group, and classroom settings

"This book offers teenagers empathetic, honest, and clear ways to challenge self-esteem and build self-insight. It touches on everything from society's external, often overbearing mixed messages, which teenagers encounter daily, to deep, personal internal conflicts and family dynamics. The numerous, unique activities offer teens a safe and positive space to change their thoughts and actions, ultimately helping them to have more successful relationships and high school careers."

> —**Nicole Brown, MAAT, LPC, CYI**, The Child, Adolescent, and Family Recovery Center and the Child, Adolescent, and Family Development Center

"Lisa Schab's workbook on self-esteem for teens is replete with commonsense exercises and instructions that are all informed by current research and developmental theory. Each of the 'Know This' prefaces illustrate Schab's practical wisdom and advanced clinical skills as a psychotherapist and professional whose knowledge-sets span the emotions, minds, and behaviors of both teens and their families."

—**Randolph Lucente, PhD**, professor of adolescent psychology at Loyola University Chicago's School of Social Work

"*The Self-Esteem Workbook for Teens* provides a comprehensive, usable format of step-by-step progression toward a healthy self-concept, the foundation of effective learning. Lisa Schab has developed a program designed to encourage self-reflection, self-awareness, perseverance, and the importance of taking action to improve the situation. Throughout, teens are counseled to pay attention to and act upon the urgings of the authentic self—an incredibly valuable life skill. The workbook could easily be used by either individuals or groups."

—**Nancy Hanrahan, MA, NCC**, school counselor at St. Joseph School, Libertyville, IL

"Adolescence is often a bewildering time when self-esteem gets battered. Teens regularly second-guess themselves and worry about their self-worth, leading them to engage in self-destructive behaviors. This workbook gives readers practical, creative, and empowering tools to not only explore their identity but build self-confidence and make smart, healthy decisions. It also helps teens become critical consumers, discover their passions, navigate peer pressure, and become more compassionate toward themselves and others. It's truly a must-read for any teen!"

—**Margarita Tartakovsky, MS**, associate editor at psychcentral.com

"This workbook encompasses all aspects of a teen's journey to a higher self-esteem."

—**Tracey Engdahl**, juvenile corrections counselor

the self-esteem workbook for teens

activities to help you build confidence and achieve your goals

LISA M. SCHAB, LCSW

Instant Help Books
An Imprint of New Harbinger Publications, Inc.

Distributed in Canada by Raincoast Books

Copyright © 2013 by Lisa M. Schab
     Instant Help Books
     An Imprint of New Harbinger Publications, Inc.
     5674 Shattuck Avenue
     Oakland, CA 94609
     www.newharbinger.com

Cover design by Amy Shoup

Library of Congress Cataloging-in-Publication Data

Schab, Lisa M.
 The self-esteem workbook for teens : activities to help you build confidence and achieve your goals / Lisa M. Schab, LCSW.
   pages cm
 ISBN 978-1-60882-582-0 (pbk. : alk. paper) -- ISBN 978-1-60882-584-4 (pdf e-book) -- ISBN 978-1-60882-583-7 (epub) 1. Self-esteem in adolescence. I. Title.
 BF724.3.S36S33 2013
 155.5'19--dc23

          2013009844

Printed in the United States of America

15 14 13

10 9 8 7 6 5 4 3 2 1

First Printing

contents

to parents and helping professionals

The purpose of this book is to help teens—both those at risk and those simply traveling through an average adolescence—to develop or enhance a state of healthy self-esteem. This condition of healthy self-esteem is understood as a positive regard for oneself, including an understanding and acceptance of one's weaknesses, a celebration of one's strengths, and a realistic conviction regarding one's equality to others. Teens with healthy self-esteem are able to know and accept themselves, practice compassion for both self and others, act with integrity and self-discipline, and use healthy coping skills, both cognitively and behaviorally, to meet life challenges. They are convinced of their unconditional worth despite changing external circumstances, and they also are convinced of and respect the worth of others.

The activities in this book are designed to help adolescents explore, understand, and value their authentic and unique selves and to teach them skills that will enable them to mature and move down their own paths with confidence, integrity, and peace.

There has been some thought that addressing self-esteem with teens may create problems related to obsessive self-focus, a sense of entitlement and superiority, overinflated ego, and a sore lack of real-world coping skills. I believe that these are characteristics not of *healthy* self-esteem, but rather the lack of it. The goal of this book is to help develop emotionally healthy people who can contribute balance, cooperation, and stability to their world—people who can work together with their fellow human beings to make positive contributions to the state of our existence.

The roller coaster of physical, emotional, and cognitive transformation that drives adolescence creates fertile ground for self-doubt and insecurity and presents the perfect time to nurture this issue while the teen is so intensely desirous of self-worth.

Thank you for your dedication to the teens in your life.

Lisa M. Schab, LCSW

introduction

Dear Reader,

Welcome to the first page of an important journey—the journey to yourself. In this book you will find activities that help you get to know who you are, understand how you came to be that person, and explore who you still want to become. You will be presented with the concept of self-worth and asked to believe that you have just as much worth as any other person on this planet.

Some of the activities will help you understand what outside factors affect your thoughts, feelings, and behaviors. Others will help you explore who you are at your core—the authentic you—before you are influenced by anyone or anything else.

You will learn ways to stay true to your authentic self, even when faced with outside pressures. You will acquire a significant number of tools to help you make your way through your life successfully, realizing positive outcomes through the thoughts you think and the choices you make.

An underlying premise of this book is: *You are okay just the way you are*. This is a basic tenet of healthy self-esteem: that we accept ourselves unconditionally—weaknesses, strengths, everything—no matter what. Some activities will help you work on this concept. Others will help you identify and focus on your "positives" so you have something to celebrate on the days when it's hard to believe that you really are okay.

Accepting every part of ourselves doesn't mean we don't try to improve or grow. You will also find activities that teach you how to gain inner strength, handle challenges better, and achieve your goals. Reading and repeating the affirmations at the end of each activity will help the concepts become reality for you.

My hope is that you will learn to understand, accept, and embrace the truth of your inherent value as a living being. Because when you actually comprehend your equality to all other beings, you can open yourself to your own love and acceptance. And that is the foundation of healthy self-esteem.

Whatever you are feeling right now, know that you have the courage to begin this amazing journey. Be open to the adventure. I wish you the very best.

Lisa M. Schab, LCSW

what healthy self-esteem means

know this

Having healthy self-esteem means you have a strong sense of self-worth. You understand and accept your weaknesses, and you appreciate and celebrate your strengths. When you have healthy self-esteem, you recognize the inborn value of all people, including yourself.

When Kati was younger, she thought everyone else was better than her—more attractive, more popular, more talented, and smarter. She felt like she never measured up, like she just wasn't good enough.

One day she saw her neighbor Tom practicing karate. Kati had always looked up to Tom; he could talk to anyone and always seemed at ease. She watched how peaceful and focused he was as he moved, and how strong he seemed, both physically and mentally.

"You are so smart and cool and confident," Kati told Tom. "I've always wished I could be like you. I get upset, I make mistakes, I say dumb things."

Tom put his arm around Kati and smiled. "Everyone gets upset, makes mistakes, and says dumb things sometimes. Everyone has fears and faults and insecurities—you just may not see them from the outside. Did you know I was so shy in grade school that I cried every morning before I got on the bus? And that I practice karate to manage anxiety?"

"But I thought you were so together!" Kati said.

"I'm human, just like you," Tom said. "You're just overly focused on your own imperfections and others' strengths, and you're basing your self-worth on that. We all come into this world the same, Kati. When you realize how equal everyone is, you'll feel better about yourself. Accept yourself and everyone else—we're all valuable, no matter what."

try this

People with healthy self-esteem are certain enough of all people's value that they can admit their faults without feeling ashamed and celebrate their strengths without putting others down.

For each of the following conversations, and check the reply you think illustrates the healthiest self-esteem:

"Congratulations on winning the freestyle swim relay!"

☐ "Thanks, it feels good. And you won the diving competition—that's great!"

☐ "I don't know why I won. I don't have good form."

☐ "Yeah, I made those other swimmers look like tadpoles!"

"I hear Patrick broke up with you. How are you feeling?"

☐ "Couldn't be better. I was planning to dump him anyway. He was dragging me down."

☐ "I figured it would happen. No one sticks with me once they get to know me."

☐ "I was pretty sad for a while, but I'm better now."

"Excuse me, but I think you're in the wrong seat. Could you check your ticket?"

☐ "Oh, sorry! I always mess things up!"

☐ "Excuse me, but I was here first. Why don't you find an empty seat?"

☐ "You're right; I apologize. I'm supposed to be in the row behind."

"Hey, that's my sweater. You didn't ask if you could borrow it!"

☐ "Sorry. You weren't home, but I should have asked you first."

☐ "Quit whining. It looks better on me anyway."

☐ "I don't know what I was thinking. It doesn't even look good on me. I'll give you one of mine to make up for it."

4

now try this

Name someone you know who appears to be "perfect."

_____

List some of that person's imperfections or challenges.

_____

_____

Describe yourself from a perspective of unhealthy self-esteem, ignoring your strengths, emphasizing your imperfections, and thinking that others are better than you.

_____

_____

_____

Describe yourself from a perspective of healthy self-esteem, recognizing your strengths, accepting your imperfections, and knowing that all people have equal value.

_____

_____

_____

today's affirmation

No matter what our strengths or weaknesses, we all have value, including me.

2 your story

know this

Everyone has a story, and everyone's story is important. It doesn't matter who your friends are, where you go to school, what your grades are, or whether your life is what you want it to be. Your story is yours alone.

You all are who you are today as a result of everything that has happened to you. Every event of your lives, every person you've met, every experience you've had has helped contribute to who we are right at this moment.

Each person's story is unique. Even if we live in the same town, go to the same school, or are in the same family, we have each traveled a unique path to arrive at this place, reading this book, at this very moment.

Knowing your story is a place to start knowing yourself. Your story is your history. Exploring it helps you understand how you came to be who you are. Telling your story allows you to honor it, and to honor and respect yourself. You deserve that, even if you don't believe it right now.

Your unique story carries information about what has happened to you. It also carries feelings, both positive and negative. Telling your story is a way to explore, recognize, and honor your life. It gives you a chance to start becoming comfortable looking inside yourself and seeing who you are.

try this

On a separate sheet of paper, make a list of significant memories from your life; for example, starting or changing schools, meeting or losing a friend, the birth of a sibling, achievements or losses, weddings or divorces, travels, and happy or difficult times. Next to each event, write the age you were when it occurred.

Write a zero at the left end of the horizontal line below. Write your current age at the right end. Transfer the items from your list to this timeline, placing each according to when it occurred. Write the age you were next to each event. If you are noting a positive memory, write it above the line. If you are noting a negative memory, write it below the line. If all your information doesn't fit, create your timeline on a separate piece of paper.

When you are done, look back at your timeline. Describe any observations or feelings you have.

_____

_____

_____

_____

_____

now try this

Now tell your story in actual story form. (Do this on other paper or at the keyboard so you have as much space as you need.) This is not an English assignment; there are no rules for composition, spelling, or grammar. Just let your story flow in whatever way it comes. You might begin with "Once upon a time …"; "I was born on …"; or "My earliest memory is …."

You might simply provide details about the life events on your timeline, or you could include more information about your birth; your family members; your different homes, schools, teachers, or other influential people; friends; vacations; or anything else that is part of your history. Your story can be as long or short as you like.

When you are done, read your story aloud to someone you trust. Describe what it felt like to write and share your personal life story.

_____

_____

_____

today's affirmation

My personal story is unique and important, and so am I.

---

know this

It doesn't matter who you are, where you have been, or what path you have taken. It doesn't matter what you have done or not done, said or not said, thought or not thought. Today, right now, you have positive qualities. Discovering them, acknowledging them, and embracing them are steps toward healthy self-esteem.

Maya's life seemed to get worse every day. Her classes were too hard this year; she couldn't keep up. Her best friend rarely talked to her anymore; she felt lonely. Her brother had won yet another award; she would never be as talented as he was. And last week she had been caught shoplifting some makeup. The store manager didn't press charges because he knew her family, but he did call her parents to tell them. Maya felt like such a loser, like she didn't fit in anywhere.

When her dad knocked on her bedroom door that day, Maya cringed. Here comes a lecture, *she thought.* And I'll be grounded for life. *But Maya's dad didn't ground her. He said that he was worried. He said that Maya was really hard on herself, and that he often heard her put herself down. Maya's dad told her she deserved to celebrate all the wonderful things about herself instead of always focusing on the things she didn't like.*

"But there is nothing good about me," said Maya. "All I do is mess up over and over again."

"If that's what you want to believe, you'll never be happy," her dad said. "Do you ever think about what a good artist you are or how much your mom and I love you? About your friends who have stuck by you since grade school? About why the Meyers ask you to babysit so often or how helpful you are to Mom when she has to work weekends? You have wonderful, positive qualities, Maya. You just don't see them because you're so busy focusing on what you don't like about yourself."

try this

Describe a time when you may have felt like Maya did. What was going on in your life?

_____

_____

Person after person can point out your positive qualities, but no one can make you believe. Deciding what you will focus on about yourself is your choice. Describe how you feel when you focus on things you don't like about yourself.

_____

_____

Describe how you feel when you focus on things you do like about yourself.

_____

_____

Sometimes our brains play tricks and try to tell us that our positives aren't real or that someone who gives us a compliment is lying. Does this ever happen to you? If so, give an example.

_____

_____

Think about deciding which of your thoughts you will choose to believe. Would you consider changing from focusing on the things you don't like about yourself to the things you do like? Tell why or why not.

_____

_____

now try this

Positives aren't all about what you win or achieve. They are also about what you attempt, what you think, and who you are. Just reading this book is a positive. It means you are willing to try something new. It means you have hope and courage and are open to change.

Circle any of the following positives that are true about you.

good listener	loyal	honest
kind to animals	talented at a sport	reliable
good sense of humor	hardworking	smart
patient	kind to people	good friend
sincere	loving	brave
clean	responsible	talented at a hobby

Give examples of each of the positives you circled; for example, if you circled "patient," describe a specific time when you expressed patience, or tell about the circumstances when you usually notice yourself acting with patience.

_____

_____

Ask three or more people what they would name as your positives and record their answers below.

_____   _____   _____

_____   _____   _____

today's affirmation

I recognize and accept my positive qualities.

11

4   brain chemical messages

Our brains are amazing and complex organs. They are the computer centers of our bodies. They regulate and maintain everything our bodies do, including influencing our self-esteem.

Different parts of the brain have different functions. For example, the deep limbic system sets the emotional tone of the mind. It influences our ability to see things in a positive or negative light. When the deep limbic system is working too hard, we tend to be negatively focused. This can lower self-esteem. Another part of the brain is the basal ganglia system, which affects our level of anxiety and nervousness. Excessive activity in this area can contribute to unfounded feelings of being judged or scrutinized. The prefrontal cortex regulates attention and organizational skills; the cingulate system affects flexibility and cooperation; and the temporal lobes affect memory, emotional stability, and aggression. Overly heightened or diminished activity in any area can affect our behavior and the way we feel about ourselves.

Along with the various systems, our brains also function with the help of chemicals, or neurotransmitters. The amount of these chemicals and their movement patterns affect our moods, perceptions, and behaviors. For example, the chemical serotonin contributes to feelings of well-being and happiness. Dopamine is associated with the brain's reward system and provides motivation. Norepinephrine affects our attention and focus. Excessively low or high levels of any of these neurotransmitters may increase our vulnerability to depression.

The physiology of our newborn brains is an inheritance from our parents. When we understand what we brought into the world genetically, we know more about what we are working with to create healthy self-esteem.

try this

Your Name

Create a "genetic family tree" by filling in the picture with information about family members who came before you. Write the names of your parents, grandparents, and great-grandparents above if possible. Add names of aunts, uncles, and cousins if you can. Under each name, write a word or two describing the person's basic personality traits. Use the words below, or choose your own.

Note: If you don't know enough about your relatives, you might ask other family members for input. However, you should respect the privacy of anyone who is not comfortable sharing information.

anxious	optimistic	overbearing	extroverted	fearful
happy-go-lucky	artistic	quirky	funny	brave
eccentric	loner	social	aggressive	rebellious
addicted	laid-back	introverted	perfectionist	passive
depressed	moody	loud	intellectual	industrious
creative	high-strung	high-achieving	lazy	rigid
pessimistic	shy	quiet	spiritual	adventurous

now try this

Looking over the picture you just created, answer these questions:

Which relatives do you think your personality is most similar to?

_____

Which relatives do you think your personality is least similar to?

_____

Which relatives do people say your personality reminds them of, and why?

_____

Describe any personality patterns you see in your family tree.

_____

Describe how you think your current self-esteem may or may not be affected by your brain chemistry.

_____

_____

Based on any influence of your genetic family history, describe areas in which you may need to work to help create healthy self-esteem for yourself.

_____

_____

today's affirmation

My current self-esteem was partly shaped by biology—
something originally beyond my control.

5 family messages

know this

How you feel about yourself today has partly to do with the messages you received as a child from people in your family. The way you interpreted those messages as a child helped you feel good or bad about yourself. When you evaluate the same messages as a young adult, you can decide which you want to keep believing and which you don't.

Dylan sat in fourth-period stress group and felt confused. Other kids had situations worse than his; it seemed they had more reason to feel stressed. He just had thoughts in his head—things he'd been told that made him feel bad about himself. But the thoughts were so loud and strong, it felt like they had the power to ruin his whole life. He felt embarrassed to bring them up to the group, so he told Ms. Chaney, the group leader, about them later.

"I keep hearing this voice in my head telling me I'm not good enough," he said. "It drives me crazy. No matter what I do, I always feel bad about myself."

"Did anyone ever actually tell you that you weren't good enough?" asked Ms. Chaney.

"Just my dad, when I was little. He always told me I should try to improve at soccer, try to imporve my grades, try to improve my attitude, try to improve everything, I guess. And even when I did get better, he would tell me to improve more."

"Your current thoughts make sense then," said Ms. Chaney. "The messages we receive as children stick with us. They are especially powerful when they come from our parents or guardians, because these are the most important people in our lives. We literally depend on them for survival. Their messages are the first ideas we have about ourselves, and they go a long way toward shaping our self-image and self-esteem.

"Ideally, we are raised by perfectly healthy people who send us only perfectly healthy messages. In reality, however, we all are raised by human beings who are doing the best they can, but are nonetheless imperfect and at any given moment may not be capable of giving healthy love or sending positive messages. What's most important to understand is that negative messages don't reflect our true worth.

"As young children, we usually believe all the messages we receive without question. As a young adult, you have the ability to look at those messages more carefully and determine which are helping you create healthy self-esteem and which aren't. You have the power to let go of any messages that aren't serving you well."

try this

Why do you think Dylan's father might have repeatedly told him to improve himself?

_____

_____

_____

_____

How do you think this felt for Dylan?

_____

_____

_____

Do you think that Dylan's father did or didn't love him?

_____

_____

_____

To create healthier self-esteem, what could Dylan do about the continued thought that he isn't good enough?

_____

_____

_____

_____

now try this

Underline any of the following messages family members may have sent you, either explicitly or by implication.

"You're not trying hard enough."

"You're not good enough."

"You'll never be able to do that."

"Why can't you be more like your brother (sister)?"

"You drive me crazy."

"Why are you doing this to me?"

"When are you going to grow up?"

"Are you stupid or something?"

"It's your fault that I'm like this."

"You could have done better."

"You don't have any right to feel angry."

"How will you ever get anywhere in life?"

"Now look what you've done."

"Can't you do anything right?"

"Let's hope you grow out of that."

Write any messages you "hear in your head" that affect your self-esteem but are not listed above.

_____

_____

_____

Tell how these messages affect how you feel about yourself today.

_____

_____

_____

On a separate piece of paper, rewrite the messages you'd like to eliminate from your mind. Put them through a shredder or rip them up and throw them away. Remind yourself that you have a choice about which messages you continue to tell yourself.

today's affirmation

I can let go of family messages that don't contribute to healthy self-esteem.

social messages   6

know this

The way you feel about yourself today has partly to do with the messages you received as a child from the society you live in. How you interpreted these messages as a child helped you feel good or bad about yourself. As a young adult, you can decide which you want to keep believing and which you don't.

Mr. Hannon's class was talking about social messages that pass on cultural beliefs. Kids were supposed to give examples from radio, TV, Internet, newspapers, and magazines.

"All I hear is ads for cars," said Max. "What's the hottest, fastest, and the best mileage."

"I look at magazines and TV and hear that everyone is supposed to be thin and beautiful," said Whitney. "It drives me crazy—I'll never look like those ads."

"Everything is about getting rich," said Jared. "There are always ads for making more money."

"I hear more and more ads for living 'green,'" said Lauren. "We're supposed to reduce, reuse, and recycle to save our environment."

"Those are all good examples," said Mr. Hannon. "The media passes on the beliefs of society. You're telling me that some things our society values are cars, beauty, money, and saving the environment.

"Now think about how you have personally been affected by those messages. How is your self-esteem affected if you do or don't have or do the things society says are valuable and acceptable?"

try this

What TV shows did you watch as a child?

_____

What messages did these shows send about what your society valued?

_____

What were the beliefs about the "best" way to look and dress?

_____

What commercials do you remember seeing?

_____

What did these commercials tell you about what your society valued?

_____

Even if you didn't understand it then, what do you remember hearing about political issues?

_____

What do you remember learning in school about what your society accepted and valued?

_____

Reading back over your answers to these questions, describe how any of those social messages may have influenced who you are or how you feel about yourself today.

_____

Which messages would you like to continue having influence over you? Which ones would you like to stop believing?

_____

now try this

If you could create your own society, what would it be like?

_____

_____

_____

What messages would you send to children to help them develop healthy self-esteem?

_____

_____

_____

Tell how your life might have been the same or different if you had received these messages as a child.

_____

_____

_____

Read these messages to yourself in front of the mirror.

today's affirmation

I don't have to believe all the messages that society feeds me.

7 self-messages

know this

The way you feel about yourself today has partly to do with messages you receive from yourself. These messages help you feel good or bad about yourself. When you identify, explore, and evaluate these messages, you can decide which you want to keep and which you don't. You can learn new ways to talk to yourself that help you develop healthy self-esteem.

Whether or not you open your mouth to speak, you actually "talk" to yourself all day long. There is a running dialogue inside your head, an inner voice sending you messages that affect how you feel about ourselves.

I shouldn't have said that ... That was an awesome movie ... I really like her ... He's so rude ... I hate this class ... I can't believe I failed again ... This tastes awful. The messages go on and on. Those that we tell about ourselves help create our self-esteem.

When Skylar makes a mistake in a band concert, she tells herself I wish I hadn't done that, but I improved overall and that's awesome! *When she doesn't have a date for the dance, she tells herself* I still have great friends to spend the night with. *Her positive self-messages help create healthy self-esteem.*

When Steven makes a mistake in a band concert, he tells himself I'll never be good at this. *When he doesn't have a date for the dance, he tells himself* No one will ever go out with me. *His negative self-messages help create unhealthy self-esteem.*

You have been telling yourself messages since you were a young child, although you weren't necessarily aware of them. As a young adult, you now have the ability to explore and pay attention to these self-messages. Then you can decide which to keep and which to let go of.

try this

Think about the messages you have sent yourself throughout the course of your life. If you can't remember exactly, take a guess. What did you tell yourself when you:

Fell off your bike when you were first learning to ride?

_____

Had a hard time learning something in school?

_____

Were rejected by a friend?

_____

Didn't get the ball through the basketball hoop?

_____

Were reprimanded by your parents?

_____

Made a mistake?

_____

Weren't picked first for a team?

_____

Over the next few days, listen for your self-messages. Notice the responses you give yourself to situations that occur during the day. Record your messages in the chart below, keeping track of how many times you use them, and circle whether they make your self-esteem go up, go down, or stay the same.

Self-Message	Number of Times Used	Self-Esteem		
		Up	Down	Same
		Up	Down	Same
		Up	Down	Same
		Up	Down	Same
		Up	Down	Same
		Up	Down	Same
		Up	Down	Same
		Up	Down	Same
		Up	Down	Same
		Up	Down	Same

Circle any of these words that describe your self-messages. Use the blank lines to add your own words.

positive	demeaning	fair	gentle	_____
harsh	compassionate	rude	offensive	_____
kind	caring	irrational	loving	_____
rational	negative	considerate	unfair	_____

How do your self-messages compare to the messages you would send to a friend?

better   the same   worse

now try this

Write five messages you could send yourself to help create healthy self-esteem.

1._____

2._____

3._____

4._____

5._____

Choose any of the following ways to send yourself each of these messages, and then follow through.

- Say this message out loud to yourself in front of a mirror.

- Send yourself this message in a text.

- Send yourself this message in an e-mail.

- Put this message on a sticky note where you will frequently see it.

- Write this message in your assignment book.

- Send yourself this message on a social networking site.

- Leave yourself this message on your voice mail.

- Write this message to yourself and mail it through the post office.

today's affirmation

I choose self-messages that help me create healthy self-esteem.

8 the truth about human worth

know this

Every human being who ever lived came into this world with value and worth. There has never been an exception. This includes you.

There may be times when you believe you are flawed. You may think other people have value and worth but for some reason you don't. You may think that somewhere deep inside, you are just wrong.

It's hard to have healthy self-esteem when we believe so strongly in our defectiveness. A belief like this colors our outlook on everything—our relationships, our accomplishments, our activities—like a shadow constantly hovering over us.

It is important to understand that this belief is false. It may seem true, but in this case, we cannot trust our thoughts. In fact, there is no human being without value and worth. There are not two rooms in the hospital nursery—one for babies born with value and one for babies born worthless. We all arrive as miracles. It is only our thoughts that tell us otherwise.

try this

Think about any newborn baby you've ever met. If you don't know any, imagine one. Imagine that tiny child, newly arrived, taking its first breaths, completely helpless and dependent on its caregivers. Think about the miracle of its birth, and think about its innocence. Check any of the statements that a medical professional might tell this baby's parents.

☐ "This baby isn't as good as the others."

☐ "It appears this child has no value."

☐ "You've created a human being with no worth."

☐ "This infant has absolutely no potential."

☐ "This child is wrong."

☐ "Your baby appears to be worthless."

It might sound absurd to think of a doctor making any of these claims about a child. And it is. It is just as absurd to think any of these statements about yourself. You were that newborn infant at one time, and your value has not disappeared over time.

In the frame below, draw or paste a picture of yourself as a newborn. Write your full name on the line underneath.

_____

Copy this statement: "Unconditional, intrinsic human worth exists constantly despite changing achievements, failures, or external circumstances."

_____

_____

_____

now try this

List situations in which you have thought of yourself as worthless or flawed.

_____

_____

Write what you told yourself at these times.

_____

_____

Give any factual, verifiable information that could confirm that you actually have no value; for example, this was printed on your birth certificate, and you have a copy of it.

_____

Tell why you think you have come to believe that you are worthless or flawed.

_____

_____

Using your own words, write a commitment to yourself to stop believing that lie.

_____

_____

_____

_____

today's affirmation

I have the same innate value and worth as every child born into this world.

9 the perfection of diversity

know this

You are genetically programmed to be yourself—and only yourself. This means you can be successful only by following your own path and becoming the best possible you.

When we aren't happy with ourselves, we may look at other people and wish we were like them. We might even try to become more like them. When we do this, we set ourselves up to fail. One human being can no more become another than an eagle can become a flamingo or a towering evergreen can become an oak.

The natural state of the universe is variety and diversity. The multitudes of species of trees, insects, birds, flowers, and animals all confirm this truth. Likewise, there are different shapes, sizes, and colors of human beings. This rich diversity exists for a purpose. There are supposed to be differences between us so that every task in nature gets accomplished. There are supposed to be different kinds of plant life and animal life—and human life.

Each individual human being is a unique combination of cells, genes, ideas, feelings, talents, and skills. To be successful in life, we must recognize, celebrate, and follow our own unique paths. Even if we devote all our energy to trying to become someone else—perhaps someone we think is "better" than us—we will only fail. Only when we try to be our own best selves can we find healthy self-esteem.

try this

Describe what might happen if there were only one type of plant in the world.

_____

_____

Describe what might happen if there were only one type of animal.

_____

_____

Think of someone you sometimes wish you were. If you spent every ounce of your energy for every day of your life trying to become that person, could you succeed?

_____

_____

What would happen in the world if everyone had the same set of talents and skills?

_____

_____

What would happen if everyone had the same job?

_____

_____

What would happen if everyone looked alike?

_____

_____

now try this

Draw a scene from an imagined world where all life forms are alike. Include plants, animals, humans, insects, or whatever you like. Remember to make all forms in each category look alike.

Look at your picture, and describe your thoughts and feelings about a world like this.

_____

_____

_____

Now draw a scene from the real world, but draw it *without* diversity. For example, maybe in real life you have a mellow black Lab and an energetic terrier as pets. In your picture, both your pets would have to be the same. In real life, you might have an athletic friend you enjoy sports with and another friend with a great sense of humor whom you love watching movies with. In your picture, both your friends would have to be the same.

Look at this picture, and describe your thoughts and feelings about a world like this.

_____

_____

_____

today's affirmation

Being myself brings success; trying to be someone else brings failure.

10 about bodies

know this

Your physical body has nothing to do with your worth. It is a miraculous container for you to live in on the planet Earth. Everyone gets one, everyone has to maintain one, and everyone's will eventually wear out. No exceptions.

Tara came home from the gymnastics meet feeling great. She had received her highest score on the trampoline, and she'd also aced her chemistry test that morning. She picked up a fashion magazine and got comfortable, wanting to relax before starting homework. But after only a few minutes, she felt her happiness dissolving. Tara was looking at swimsuit ads. The models were all far thinner and taller than she was, and they all had perfect skin. They all looked carefree and happy, and all had handsome guys at their sides. Who cares what I do on the tramp or in school? *she thought.* I'll never look like that.

The next day in assembly, a guest speaker described how photos of models are prepared for publication. With one touch on a keyboard, she made eyes wider, thighs thinner, and muscles more toned. "It's important to know that what we see in ads is not reality; the images have almost all been retouched," she said.

The speaker also talked about the big business of bodies. "Billions of dollars are spent each year to keep us believing that the most important aspect of our bodies is the way they look. And that if we look a particular way, our lives will be happy and problem-free. If we buy into this idea, we also buy beauty and diet products, so the industry makes a lot of money. When the models aren't even 'real,' we can never match them, so we never stop buying. But we have a choice. We don't have to be controlled by a business. We can think for ourselves and remember that our inner qualities are more valuable than our measurements. We can be grateful that our awesome bodies are working for us at every moment."

She went on to talk about how easy it is to forget the true purposes of our bodies: to see, hear, swallow, think, touch, digest, rest, heal, taste, take in fuel, move from place to place, and reproduce ourselves. "We forget about these miracles when we focus on looks," she said. "We also damage our self-esteem when we buy into the false belief that our value is connected to how we look and that we would be happy if only we were taller, shorter, thinner, more or less muscular, clear-skinned, fair-skinned, or darker skinned, or if we had different clothes."

Tara thought about how her body had been so loyal to her at the gymnastics meet and how her brain had worked for her in the chemistry test. She decided it wasn't worth the energy of hating her body or her looks.

try this

In these frames, paste a picture of yourself as a child and a picture of yourself today.

Bodies naturally change over time. List the changes you see in the pictures. Then, underline any change that affects your intrinsic worth as a human being.

_____

_____

_____

These words and phrases describe parts of your physical body. Next to each, write its purpose. Put a star next to those for which you are grateful.

_____ veins	_____ elbows	_____ leg bones
_____ lungs	_____ eyeballs	_____ fingers
_____ heart	_____ eardrums	_____ teeth
_____ kneecaps	_____ skin	_____ nostrils
_____ toenails	_____ nipples	_____ navel
_____ digestive system	_____ taste buds	_____ reproductive organs

These people will be studied and remembered for generations to come. Circle those whose contribution to society had anything to do with the way they looked.

Martin Luther King	Florence Nightingale	Marie Curie
Abraham Lincoln	Mahatma Gandhi	JK Rowling
William Shakespeare	Christopher Columbus	Thomas Edison
Albert Einstein	Nelson Mandela	Julius Caesar
Mother Teresa	Eleanor Roosevelt	Galileo

Describe the most important thing you would want people to remember as your contribution to the world. (Would it be your looks? A positive change you made for society? Love or caring you gave to others? How you helped someone less fortunate? A career achievement? Something else?)

_____

_____

_____

now try this

Over the next few days, record the media messages you hear about bodies. Circle the T next to those that are true, and circle the dollar sign next to those created to make money.

T $ _____

T $ _____

T $ _____

T $ _____

T $ _____

T $ _____

T $ _____

T $ _____

T $ _____

Tell how the dollar-sign messages affect your self-esteem.

_____

_____

_____

today's affirmation

I refuse to let a business tell me the worth of my human body.

know this

Every human being is imperfect, including you. Perfection is literally impossible, and you, like everyone else, are set up to make mistakes. You will continue making mistakes as long as you are alive. This has nothing to do with your worth.

When Jack heard the buzzer, he wished he could disappear through the gym floor. He had missed the final shot and lost the division game for his team. For the whole school. For the whole town! He walked off the court and into the locker room, hoping to leave before anyone found him.

As the rest of his team came in, they patted Jack on the back and congratulated him on a good game. "Don't worry, we've got next year," one said. But he could sense their disappointment. He hated himself for letting them down. He picked up his duffel bag without bothering to shower or change. He just had to get out of there.

He heard Coach Anderson call, "Hey Jack, let's talk." Coach put his arm around Jack's shoulders and headed him toward the parking lot. The two of them got into Coach's car.

"I really don't want to talk," Jack said. "I feel bad enough already."

"Then just listen," said Coach. He told Jack a story of how in college he had missed the same shot in the playoffs and felt like he could never face his team again.

"You?" Jack said. "But you're a fantastic player and an awesome coach!"

"We all mess up sometimes. Making mistakes is part of being human. Ever notice that every computer keyboard has a delete key? They don't just hand those out to certain people. Everyone gets them, automatically, because everyone makes mistakes.

"If you choose to see each mistake as a normal part of life, and a chance to learn and grow, you automatically turn it into something positive. As the story goes, when Thomas Edison tried over 900 times to create a working light bulb, someone asked him how he felt about his failures. Edison said, 'I didn't fail—I just found 899 ways not to make a light bulb.'"

try this

On a separate sheet of paper, keep a record of human beings making mistakes. Maybe your little brother trips when he is running; maybe your dad spills his coffee; maybe you see a car accident. Human mistakes are boundless. See how long it takes to witness a hundred mistakes, including your own.

now try this

Change your thoughts to change your feelings about yourself. First, make a list of any negative thoughts you have when you make a mistake.

_____

_____

_____

Now cross out those statements and write new, positive self-messages that will help you accept imperfection and feel better about yourself.

_____

_____

_____

Think about a mistake you made recently that you got down on yourself for. Close your eyes, take a few cleansing breaths, and relax. Now picture yourself making that same mistake, but responding with healthy self-esteem. Imagine what you would do and say differently. Imagine treating yourself with the compassion and rational thinking that is a part of healthy self-esteem.

today's affirmation

My goal is not to stop making mistakes; my goal is to use them to learn and grow.

12 about comparing

know this

Healthy self-esteem is not contingent on comparisons. It exists no matter what other people are achieving or not achieving. Healthy self-esteem can grow stronger when we stop comparing our unique selves to other people.

You might get your report card and think you aren't as smart as your sibling. You might think kids you know are more attractive, or have more confidence, money, friends, or talents, and always feel bad about yourself in comparison.

Or, you might see someone at school who struggles socially and think you're more popular. You might see your friend's lower test grade and feel glad you did better. You might look at people who are less attractive, live in different neighborhoods, get into more trouble, or don't fit in, and you might feel good about yourself in comparison.

Comparing ourselves to others might raise or lower our self-esteem temporarily. But the rise or drop isn't realistic, because as soon as we compare ourselves to yet another person, our feelings can change again. If our self-esteem fluctuates with whom we are comparing ourselves to, it isn't truly healthy.

try this

On the left, write the names of three people you compare yourself to who make you feel better about yourself. Then circle a number on the self-esteem scale to show how you feel about yourself in comparison to these people.

On the right, write the names of three people you compare yourself to who make you feel worse about yourself. Then circle a number on the self-esteem scale to show how you feel about yourself in comparison to these people.

1. _____   1. _____

2. _____   2. _____

3. _____   3. _____

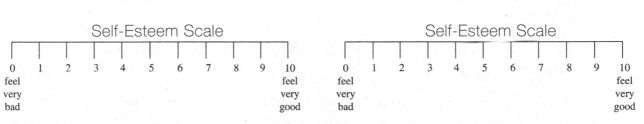

If you recorded different levels of self-esteem on each scale, tell why. Then explain how these comparisons don't create truly healthy self-esteem.

_____

_____

_____

now try this

Mark these statements true or false.

_____ My value as a human being actually changes when I compare myself to one person versus another.

_____ I am a more valuable person when I compare myself to others and my self-esteem rises.

_____ I am a less valuable person when I compare myself to others and my self-esteem drops.

_____ My thoughts about myself change when I compare myself to one person versus another.

_____ My feelings about myself change when I compare myself to one person versus another.

_____ My true value as a human being remains the same even when I compare myself to other people.

_____ My true value as a human being remains the same whether I think thoughts that contribute to healthy self-esteem or unhealthy self-esteem.

Try going through one day without comparing yourself to others. Comparison thoughts will still come into your mind, but when you notice them, try to respond differently. You might try to consciously block them, change them, or just let them exist without buying into them.

Tell what it was like to try to stop comparing.

_____

_____

_____

How do you think you would feel about yourself if you were able to completely stop comparing yourself to others?

_____

_____

_____

today's affirmation

My value doesn't change when I compare myself to others.

13 about judgment

know this

Human beings often judge each other because it helps them temporarily feel better about themselves. People who put you down might think they are better than you. If you put others down, you might think you are better than them. But it's not true. Self-worth exists as a truth, independent of any outside judgments. When we have healthy self-esteem, we recognize that and don't need to judge others or let their judgments bother us.

Maggie and some friends were standing by her locker. When Cori walked by, two of the girls rolled their eyes. "Can you believe her?" one asked. "How could she wear something like that to school?"

"She's crazy," said another. "What do you expect?"

In science class, Maggie overheard some kids making rude comments about a particular minority. They were making fun of them, making generalizations, and being critical of people they didn't know.

That night at a party, Maggie's good friend Zach called her selfish when Maggie said she wouldn't lie to his girlfriend for him. Maggie felt really upset and left. When she got home, her mother could tell something was wrong and asked what had happened.

"I'm tired of people judging each other so negatively," said Maggie. "Why do we do that? We say such mean and unfair things about other people all the time." She told her mom about the three situations.

"People usually make judgments to feel better about themselves," said Maggie's mom. "When we criticize someone else's looks or lifestyle, somewhere deep inside we think, I'm not as bad as that. *Or, sometimes we are feeling negative and unfairly let it out on another person.*

"Your girlfriends and the kids in class may feel superior when they talk that way about others. Zach may have felt frustrated about the problems with his girlfriend, or guilty because he knew he shouldn't ask you to lie for him. He was covering up his real feelings by criticizing you. That's why it's important not to take those judgments personally. Judging says more about the person doing the judging than about the one being judged."

48

try this

Judging others doesn't make us any better than them; it doesn't make us right and them wrong; it doesn't make us more valuable and them less valuable. All judging does is make us feel temporarily (and falsely) better about ourselves.

For one day, pay attention to the judgmental statements you hear from people in the following categories. Try to find and record at least two in each category.

Family

_____

_____

Friends

_____

_____

Acquaintances

_____

_____

Strangers

_____

_____

Myself

_____

_____

Do any of these judgments actually make the criticisms true?

_____

49

Explain why the following speakers may have made these judgments:

"She's stuck up because she's in all honors classes. She's probably boring because all she does is study."

_____

_____

_____

"The people who live over there are awful. I'm glad I'm not one of them."

_____

_____

_____

"He's really handsome, but girls probably just use him because they want to be seen with a cute guy."

_____

_____

_____

"Do you always have to be in such a good mood? It's so irritating."

_____

_____

_____

now try this

Try going through one day without judging others. When you notice judgmental thoughts, try to replace them with accepting thoughts. Describe two specific examples of situations in which you changed your thoughts.

1. _____

2. _____

Tell what it was like to let go of judgment.

_____

Describe a recent situation in which you heard a negative judgment about yourself.

_____

What did you tell yourself? What feelings did your thoughts create? How did this affect your self-esteem?

_____

_____

_____

_____

_____

_____

today's affirmation

Another person's judgment does not change my self-worth.

14 your authentic self

know this

Your authentic self is who you are before you change things—thoughts, feelings, looks, or actions—because you think you have to. It is who you are before you are affected by external expectations or opinions. Many of us have lost track of our authentic selves because we have tried so hard to be something else. The healthier our self-esteem, the better we can know, trust, and express our authentic selves.

Jamie's girlfriends were so into horses that they took riding lessons twice a week and volunteered at the stables in their free time. Jamie really had no interest in horses, but she pretended to like them because her friends did. She asked for riding boots for her birthday, took lessons after school, and spent her free time at the stables, too.

One day while Jamie was grooming a horse, the stable owner, Vivie, said, "You look like your mind is a million miles away! What are you thinking about?"

"Running," said Jamie. "Sign-ups for the cross-country team are today. I love running. I've always wanted to be on the team."

"Then what on earth are you doing here?" asked Vivie.

"Well, my friends are here. And I like to be with them. And it's cool to like horses ..."

"It sounds like you're here because of what other people want, not what you want," said Vivie. "You're not acting from your authentic self. How do you feel when you run, and how do you feel when you're here?"

"When I run, I feel fantastic," said Jamie. "It might sound funny, but I feel at home, like I was born to run. When I'm here, I feel ... kind of out of place—like I'm just visiting."

"That's because you are," said Vivie. "You're visiting your friends' lives. I suggest you go back to your own life and get on that team. Listen to your authentic self, and start running!"

try this

Very young children are usually still in touch with their authentic selves. They haven't yet been influenced by other people's opinions. Describe anything you can remember about what you liked to do, what you liked to play with, or whom you liked to spend time with when you were a child.

_____

_____

_____

List the elective activities you are involved in now. Rate each activity from 1 (low) to 10 (high) according to how much your authentic self wants to do it. Next to your rating, explain why you are doing it, if not for your authentic self.

Activity	AS Rating	Why I'm Doing This

Circle the AS below next to any choice you make from your authentic self. Circle the OF next to any you make because of other factors. Next to each OF choice, write what those factors are; for example, "My parents make me"; "I want to fit in"; "It's against the rules"; "We can't afford what I really want"; "It's cool.")

AS   OF   What I wear to school _____

AS   OF   What I wear outside of school _____

AS   OF   What I eat for lunch _____

AS   OF   What I do on weekends _____

AS   OF   Who my friends are _____

AS   OF   What I do during the summer _____

AS   OF   What I read _____

AS   OF   What music I listen to _____

AS   OF   How I spend my money _____

Describe what you would do differently regarding these activities if you were acting only from your authentic self.

_____

_____

_____

now try this

Place a check mark next to any of these words that you think describes you. Then circle those that describe you when you are being your authentic self. (You may both check and circle the same words.) Use the blank lines to add your own words.

unworthy	lonely	loud	flexible
critical	happy	accepting	active
assertive	anxious	compassionate	incompetent
needy	clumsy	quiet	dishonest
calm	conceited	cruel	responsible
promiscuous	rude	well-behaved	reliable
honest	busy	lazy	joyful
thoughtful	loving	talkative	discouraged
sad	bored	studious	sensitive
kind	friendly	wise	outgoing
hardworking	afraid	brave	passive
angry	creative	isolated	overwhelmed
curious	loyal	conflicted	healthy
confused	generous	empty	rigid
athletic	relaxed	peaceful	_____
selfish	smart	depressed	_____
prejudiced	confident	aggressive	_____

How do your checks and circles compare?

_____

_____

_____

What can you learn about your authentic self from this exercise?

_____

_____

_____

_____

_____

today's affirmation

I can discover and explore my authentic self.

---

know this

Being part of a family can influence the choices you make about how you think, feel, and act. You may play a certain role in your family. You may try to live up to their expectations. You may rebel against your family members or you may try to please them. Some of these decisions might be made from your authentic self; some might not.

Maddie's parents were always arguing. Sometimes their disagreements were violent, with swearing and threats and one or both of them storming out of the house. Their fighting frightened Maddie. When she was home, she spent much of her time trying to help her parents get along, but without any success.

Jackie's older brother was a star wrestler, got straight As, and was liked by everyone. Jackie felt like a loser compared to him, and she started getting into trouble at school. She didn't really want to do bad things, but at least she got attention for it, which felt better than living in her brother's shadow.

Nick's mom had been struggling financially for years, and his family was often evicted for not paying rent on time. Nick's mother relied on him to have a weekend job to help pay bills, to watch his younger brothers after school, and to cook dinner when she had to work late. Nick knew his mom and brothers depended on him, and he never let them down.

Carlos had always wanted to be a teacher. He loved teaching little kids things—from bike riding to math to how to spot shooting stars. But Carlos's parents were both attorneys, and they expected him to go to law school. Carlos took political science courses to please them, but he was more interested in the tutoring he did after school.

Family situations and expectations shape our lives and help create roles for us—the parts we play in relationship to other family members—such as "achiever," "rebel," "caretaker," "clown," or "scapegoat." Even as we become more independent, family affects our choices and behaviors, our personalities, and our self-esteem. This influence can lead us to choices that are very much in line with, or very different from, our authentic selves.

try this

On the numbered lines below, (1) tell how you think each teen might be affected by his or her family circumstances; (2) choose a role from the list below, or write your own, that might be created by each of their situations; and (3) tell why you think this role is or is not in line with each person's authentic self.

Maddie

1. _____

2. _____

3. _____

Jackie

1. _____

2. _____

3. _____

Nick

1. _____

2. _____

3. _____

Carlos

1. _____

2. _____

3. _____

clown	intellectual	critic
disciplinarian	instigator	moralist
bully	caretaker	counselor
achiever	baby	commander-in-chief
rule keeper	rebel	loser
peacemaker	neutral party	judge
scapegoat	boss	confronter
hero	goody-goody	free spirit
overachiever	tough guy	blamer

now try this

Draw all your family members, including yourself. Add their names and the role you think each plays in your family. Choose from the list above or create your own.

Tell how it feels to play the role you play in your family.

_____

_____

Describe how you think your family expects you to:

Think

_____

Talk

_____

Feel

_____

Behave

_____

Write a number from 1 (low) to 10 (high) next to each answer, rating how much you think you are your authentic self when you act to fill your family's expectations.

If your family had no expectations of you, tell which of the above you would do differently and which you would still do the same.

_____

_____

Tell how you think your relationship with your family affects your self-esteem.

_____

_____

_____

today's affirmation

Looking past the roles I play in my family, I can find my authentic self.

16 who you are for your friends

know this

Your friends can influence the choices you make about how you think, feel, and act. You may play a certain role in your peer group. You may try to live up to its expectations. You may try to fit in by pleasing your friends or identify yourself by being different. Some of these decisions might be made from your authentic self; some might not.

Maria's best friends were Amie and Hannah. They had known one another since kindergarten and had the best times together—at the mall or movies, on sleepovers or dates. But when she started playing coed volleyball, Maria got close to Noah and Emily. Maria was a strong player, and her new friends encouraged her. When she was with them, she focused solely on athletics and felt confident she could get a scholarship someday.

Having two sets of friends felt confusing sometimes. When she was with Amie and Hannah, Maria was more careful about her appearance and she talked more about boys. With Noah and Emily, she wore sweats or workout clothes, thought of herself as an athlete, and even tended to eat healthier.

Maria liked being with both sets of friends, but she began to feel like two different people.

"Which feels more like the real you?" her sister asked.

"I guess a little of each," Maria said. "I have so much fun with Amie and Hannah, but I also like focusing on sports with Noah and Emily. With one group, I'm the party girl; with the other, I'm the athlete."

"If you change because you really like each situation, you're being true to yourself," her sister said. "But if you change because you're trying to fit in, you're just playing a game. Do what's right for you. Your true friends will stick by you no matter what."

try this

In column 1 of the following chart, list one or more groups of friends to which you belong. Identify each group with a different name, such as "service club" or "neighborhood." In column 2, write the role or roles you think you play in that group. Choose from those below or write your own. In column 3, rate how comfortable you feel with that group on a scale from 1 (low) to 5 (high). In column 4, tell whether your self-esteem is high, average, or low when you are with that group.

Group	My Role	My Comfort Level	Self-Esteem Rating
			high average low
			high average low
			high average low
			high average low
			high average low

partier	daredevil	voice of reason	peacemaker
romantic	joker	instigator	connector
listener	counselor	critic	rebel
brain	planner	bully	ghost
leader	follower	victim	speaker

now try this

Give an example of how your friends influence how you think.

_____

Give an example of how your friends influence how you feel.

_____

Give an example of how your friends influence how you act.

_____

Describe the things you might do differently if you were not influenced by your friends.

_____

On the scale below, write in each group of your friends at a point that shows how far you are from your authentic self when you are with them.

my
authentic
self

nothing
at all
like my
authentic
self

today's affirmation

I can choose thoughts, feelings, and actions that come from my authentic self.

Jasmine hated her curly black hair. She straightened it whenever she could because that's what models looked like in magazines. Sometimes she wished she lived with her cousins in Puerto Rico, where curly hair was accepted and even thought of as pretty.

Marcus was the only boy who signed up for Future Nurses Club. Sometimes his guy friends would tease him, calling him Nurse Markie. Sometimes adults would say, "You mean you want to be a doctor, not a nurse, right?" He thought about dropping out, but he really liked the club. Marcus had a deep feeling that nursing was right for him. He loved helping sick people and didn't want the pressures of medical school. Sometimes he felt angry that people thought there was something wrong with guys being nurses.

Abby was raised in a strict religious community that had many rules about behavior. Abby agreed with some of the faith's values but not with others. Abby hated when people assumed she was just like the other members of her community. She was afraid to speak out about her ideas and found herself starting to break rules as a way of telling people that she was different.

Part of growing into your own identity requires exploring and discovering your own authentic ideas and ideals, your own beliefs and values. Healthy self-esteem includes having the strength and confidence to stay true to them, as long as they are safe, whether or not they go along with society's ideas.

try this

For each of the situations above, answer the following questions.

Jasmine

What social value is Jasmine affected by?

_____

How does she feel about it?

_____

What does she do about it?

_____

How do you think her self-esteem is affected by this situation?

_____

What would you do in her place?

_____

Marcus

What social value is Marcus affected by?

_____

How does he feel about it?

_____

What does he do about it?

_____

How do you think his self-esteem is affected by this situation?

_____

What would you do in his place?

_____

Abby

What social value is Abby affected by?

_____

How does she feel about it?

_____

What does she do about it?

_____

How do you think her self-esteem is affected by this situation?

_____

What would you do in her place?

_____

now try this

Circle all of the following that are sources of social pressure for you. Use the blank lines to add your own.

radio	magazines	religious leaders	_____
television	social media	teachers	_____
Internet	in-person speakers	school staff	_____
billboards	politicians	gang members	_____

Over the next few days, pay attention to and record times when you are affected by your society's ideas and values. Record how your self-esteem is affected by rating it from 1 (low) to 10 (high) in the chart below. For example, you might notice your self-esteem go up when you watch a TV show that praises a minority group you belong to. Or, you might notice your self-esteem go down if you have freckles and see an ad for a product that gets rid of "nasty" freckles.

Day/Time	Incident	Source	Self-Esteem (1-10)

Think about how your thoughts, feelings, or actions might be different if you were not affected by your society's values.

Describe any positive changes that would occur?

_____

_____

_____

_____

_____

_____

Describe any negative changes that would occur?

_____

_____

_____

_____

_____

_____

today's affirmation

I can decide to let social values influence me or not.

18 it's normal to not know

know this

If you don't know exactly who your authentic self is, what you want to do with your life, or even what you want to do next year, you are perfectly normal. Most teenagers are trying to figure these things out. It is impossible to have all of the answers right now.

Christie felt exhausted thinking about the career assembly earlier that morning. There had been representatives from different fields, from fast food to medicine. Christie had no idea what she wanted for her future; she had a hard enough time figuring out which classes to take.

"Sometimes I'm not even sure who I want to eat lunch with," she told her guidance counselor, Mr. Williams. "Some days I want the fun of my dance teammates, and sometimes I just want to sit with Ariel, who's really quiet. Some days I think I want to go to cooking school, and sometimes I want to be an accountant. What's wrong with me?"

Mr. Williams assured Christie there was absolutely nothing wrong with her. "Adolescence is a time to test your ideas and explore your interests, to try out different friendships and discover the person you are most comfortable being," he said.

"But it seems like everyone else knows who they are and what they want," Christie said. "Lacey is going to be a dentist, Beth wants to stay home and have six kids—and I'm not even sure if I want to join band or choir!"

"Lots of kids have ideas now," said Mr. Williams. "Some will stay on those paths, but many won't. The more we learn, the more we grow and change, and none of you have finished learning or growing. It can feel confusing and frustrating, or you might feel scared that you'll never figure it out. But it's important to remember that not knowing is completely normal. You can allow yourself to unfold one step at a time."

try this

Think back to when you were five. Try to remember anything you knew about yourself or desired for your future. Record what you remember below. Then do the same for every few years up until your current age.

Age 5

_____

Age _____

_____

Age _____

_____

Age _____

_____

Age _____

_____

Age _____

_____

How has your self-knowledge changed over time?

_____

_____

How have your dreams for the future changed?

_____

_____

now try this

List your ideas about yourself and your future. (For example, "I'm outgoing," "I'm going to cosmetology school," or "I'm going into politics.") Next to each statement write a number from 1 (not very certain) to 5 (very certain) to show how you feel about this idea.

_____

_____

_____

_____

_____

Fill in the blanks below, giving yourself permission to not know everything about yourself or your future.

I, _____, give myself permission to _____

_____

_____

_____

_____   _____

Date   Signature

today's affirmation

It is normal to feel uncertain about exactly what I want in my future.

---

know this

You can learn about your authentic self by looking at what you like and don't like. No one else in the world has the exact combination of preferences and dislikes as you do.

"Today we're going to learn about ourselves by exploring our likes and dislikes," said Ms. Henning, Olivia's psychology teacher. "We make hundreds of choices every day, which are in great part determined by what we like and don't like. Every choice we make determines our behavior, moves us a little further down our path, and shapes the life we are creating for ourselves. What are some choices you make on an average day?"

"Red T-shirt or brown," said Kyle.

"Bagels or cereal," said Willow.

"Watch a movie or go to the mall," said Olivia.

"Run track or play softball," said Owen.

"Our preferences come partly from experience," said Ms. Henning. "If we've done something and liked it, we want to do it again. They also come partly from biology: liking green more than yellow or hot sauce more than soy sauce. Our preferences are influenced by the way our brain and body cells react to them."

"Why are we talking about hot sauce and soy sauce?" asked Kyle.

"Good question!" said Ms. Henning, smiling. "Because becoming more aware of what we like and dislike helps us strengthen our sense of self. We get a better understanding of who we are and why."

try this

Check the item in each pair below that appeals to you the most.

walk	ride		save	discard
cook	eat out		cold	hot
write	speak		numbers	words
focus	dream		day	night
books	TV		desert	mountains
home	away		give	receive
plane	train		rock	rap
hard	soft		school	work
bath	shower		air	ground
fast	slow		jeans	sweats
formal	casual		sugar	salt
meat	veggies		city	country
comedy	drama		structure	flow
cola	clear		spring	fall
alone	together		land	sea
sandals	sneakers		play	watch
curly	straight		sitcom	news
dark	light		talk	listen

Fill in the chart below to record your most and least favorite:

	Love	Hate		Love	Hate
movie			drink		
food			game		
song			author		
color			TV show		
class			hobby		
actor			city		
sport			indulgence		
animal			book		
music			month		

now try this

If you could be any living creature other than a human, tell what you would like to be and why. Think about details. Would you like to fly, swim, run, or crawl? Would you rather live in the wild, a zoo, or someone's home or yard?

_____

_____

If you could be any food, tell what you would like to be and why. Would you like to be spicy? Sweet? Bitter? Would you be eaten hot or cold? Would you be a main course or a side dish?

_____

_____

Compare the description of your animal to your food. Do they seem to have similar qualities? If they are not similar, tell how they are different.

_____

_____

_____

Describe anything you think your choices tell you about yourself.

_____

_____

_____

today's affirmation

My personal likes and dislikes help me understand who I am.

discovering your dreams 20

---

know this

You can learn about your authentic self by exploring your dreams, ideas, and goals. Daydreams, night dreams, purposeful thoughts, and random thoughts all give you clues to who you really are and what you really want.

"Today we're going to explore our dreams," said Ms. Henning. "When we daydream about the future, we usually think about the situations or people that appeal to us most. Maybe you imagine yourself making the honor roll, going to a concert, dating someone in particular, or taking a vacation."

"I daydream about traveling somewhere with palm trees and beaches," said Willow.

"Sometimes I dream about being a vet and sometimes an engineer," said Olivia.

"I dream about living alone someday—with no brothers and sisters!" said Andrew.

"Your dreams about your future can be very clear, or they might be hazy or conflicted," said Ms. Henning. "They're often affected by the way you are growing up, or how you see adults you know living their lives. You might think you want your future to be better than your parents'. You might want to carry on family traditions or make new ones."

"I dream about helping kids with disabilities, like my sister who has Down syndrome," said Ashley.

"My dream is to play pro football instead of sitting in an office like my dad," said Kyle.

"When you explore your dreams for the future, you can learn more about who you are today," said Ms. Henning.

try this

To help identify some of your personal dreams, answer these questions:

If I could make three wishes come true, they would be:

1. _____

2. _____

3. _____

If I won the lottery, the first three things I would spend the money on would be:

1. _____

2. _____

3. _____

If I could travel anywhere in the world, I would go to:

1. _____

2. _____

3. _____

If I could have any talent or skill, it would be:

1. _____

2. _____

3. _____

Circle any of the following you would like to change about yourself:

gender	religion	ethnicity
race	country of birth	family makeup
physical abilities	social abilities	intellectual abilities

now try this

Find a quiet place where you won't be disturbed. Make yourself comfortable and close your eyes. Put your attention on your breath for a few minutes to help you clear your mind. You don't have to change your breathing pattern; just pay attention to it. Notice where your breath moves in and out and how far it travels into your body. Let yourself relax into your breathing, feeling peace within yourself. When you feel calm and safe, allow your mind to move into the future. Imagine that the date is five years from today. Think about what you would like your ideal day to be like five years from now. Pretend that you can make this day anything you want—there are no limits. Picture yourself waking up in the morning. Look around. What kind of setting are you in? What colors, sounds, and feelings do you experience? What is the first thing you do upon waking? What do you do next? What do you see? Whom do you interact with? Think about how you would spend your time all day if you could do anything you wanted. Whom you would be with? Where you would go? Take as much time as you like to imagine your entire day this way, picturing everything just the way you'd like it. When you have finished this visualization, answer these questions.

Tell where you were when you woke up on your ideal day.

_____

_____

_____

List the things you did.

_____

_____

_____

List the people you were with, if anyone.

_____

_____

_____

List the feelings you had during this day.

_____

_____

_____

What do the details you chose for your ideal day tell you about what you value and long for?

_____

_____

_____

How is your ideal day similar to what you wrote down in the previous exercise?

_____

_____

_____

today's affirmation

My dreams about the future help reveal my authentic self.

discovering your beliefs 21

know this

You can learn about your authentic self by exploring your beliefs. Your beliefs about the world, life, what is right or wrong, and what is good or bad all affect how you think, feel, and act. Some of these beliefs might reflect your authentic self; some might not.

These phrases were on the board when Olivia walked into psychology class:

How the world was created

What the drinking age should be

Whether the dress code in our school is fair

How much power the government should have

Whether there is life after death

"We all have beliefs about these topics," said Ms. Henning. "Our belief systems may be influenced by our families, our friends, our ethnic and religious traditions, and everything we learn as we grow up. Beliefs exist across all categories. They may be strong or mild, rational or irrational. They may be certain or open to change.

"Who can share some beliefs you learned as a child?"

"My family has a strong belief about education," said Bryan. "Ever since we were born, my parents have told my brothers and me that we will go to college."

"My parents say, 'Honesty is the best policy,'" said Willow.

"My dad says, 'The government should get off our backs,'" said Kyle.

"My aunt and my mom are always telling me what they say in church," said Olivia. "It's better to give than to receive."

"Those are all good examples," said Ms. Henning. "Sometimes we carry on the beliefs we are taught because we agree with them. Sometimes we continue believing them just because we never stopped to question whether they are right for us.

"Whatever your beliefs are, you have a right to them. They help you make choices about the life you are creating for yourself. When you explore your belief systems, you can understand yourself better."

try this

Make a list of the ideas or beliefs you grew up hearing repeatedly, whether from your family, friends, or society. To the left of each, circle the up arrow if you agree with this belief and the down arrow if you disagree with it.

↑ ↓ 1. _____

↑ ↓ 2. _____

↑ ↓ 3. _____

↑ ↓ 4. _____

↑ ↓ 5. _____

Rewrite any beliefs you disagree with, changing them to more accurately reflect your personal beliefs.

1. _____

2. _____

3. _____

4. _____

5. _____

Circle the number that most closely represents what percentage of time you act on beliefs that don't reflect your authentic self.

10%   20%   30%   40%   50%   60%   70%   80%   90%   100%

now try this

Choose five of the following questions to answer from your personal beliefs, not just what others have told you. Your beliefs may be the same or different from your friends' or family's. You might not be sure about your beliefs on any of these topics, and that's okay.

Which environmental issues are the most important?

_____

Which political stance makes the most sense to you: liberal, moderate, or conservative?

_____

What do you believe about war?

_____

Should it be easier or harder to get divorced?

_____

Should your state's drinking age be changed?

_____

Should your state's driving age be changed?

_____

Would wearing school uniforms help students feel more equal to each other?

_____

Under what circumstances is it okay to have sex?

_____

Is spanking children okay?

_____

Is there a God?

_____

What happens to people after they die?

_____

How was human life created?

_____

Should abortion be legal?

_____

Should all people have the right to own a gun?

_____

Should the death penalty be abolished?

_____

What kinds of rights or services should illegal immigrants have?

_____

Should street drugs be legalized?

_____

Should legal marriage be available for same-gender couples?

today's affirmation

My beliefs help me understand what is important to me.

discovering your passions 22

know this

You can learn about your authentic self by exploring the things you feel passionate about. You might feel passionate about ideas, possessions, activities, or people. Passion is a feeling that comes from deep within you and is usually a reflection of your authentic self.

On the final day of class, Olivia's teacher announced they would be talking about passion. Some of the students laughed. "I thought we only talked about that in health class!" someone said.

"You're thinking of sexual passion," said Ms. Henning. "That's an example of passion, but only one kind. A passion can be anything that moves you deeply, from an idea to a hobby to a person. We usually feel a strong commitment to our passions, a connection that goes beyond a thinking level. We can feel our passions physically, emotionally, and spiritually; they run stronger and deeper than likes and dislikes. Who can name a passion they have and tell how it affects them?"

"Animal rights," said Owen. "I've seen movies and read articles about how cruelly animals are treated on factory farms. Lots of them are confined to small cages and can't even stand up their whole lives. That's why I'm a vegetarian."

"Don't laugh," said Andrew, "but my passion is my baseball collection! I've got autographed baseballs from nine major leaguers, and I'm hoping to get number ten this summer. Once I found my brother playing with one, and I got really mad. They're pretty important to me."

"Dance," said Ashley. "I've taken lessons since kindergarten, and I don't know if I'll ever stop. I love how I feel when I'm dancing."

"I guess I feel passionate about my boyfriend," said Olivia. "Not only in a physical way, but I just like being with him so much. We both like skiing and horror movies and pizza with everything on it. He's kind and honest, and he makes me laugh. I guess he's my best friend."

"Good," said Ms. Henning. "You've identified that we can feel passionate about ideas, possessions, activities, and people. Identifying your passions can increase your awareness of your authentic self."

try this

Circle any of the following ideas, possessions, activities, people or animals you feel passionate about.

Ideas

politics	civil rights	religion	the arts	education
animal rights	divorce	freedom	peace	health

Possessions

jewelry	clothes	books	sports equipment	cars
money	computers	phones	works of art	music

Activities

learning	socializing	athletics	art	music	travel
volunteering	eating	sleeping	being outdoors		reading

People/Animals

my parents	my friends	my extended family	the human race	the sick
the homeless	my pets	people with disabilities	my siblings	my boy- or girlfriend

In this frame, describe your passions more personally through writing or drawing. For example, you might write someone's name or how you feel about mandatory school attendance, or draw your favorite hobby.

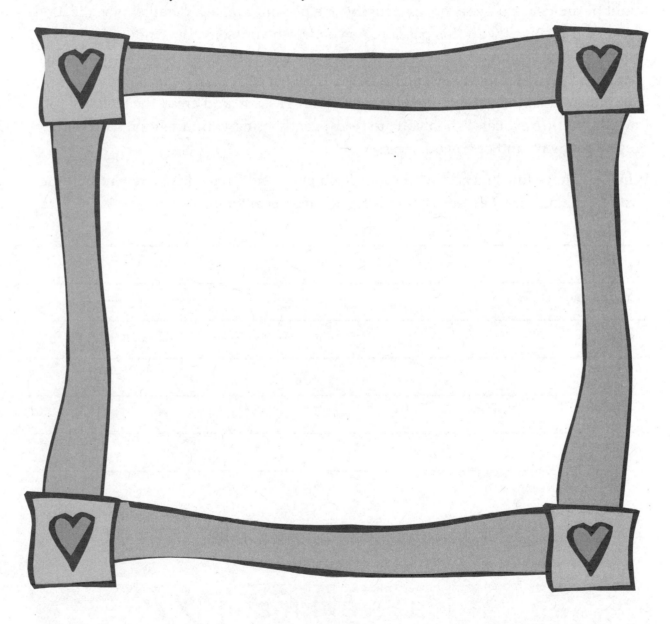

now try this

Take a few minutes to sit quietly and comfortably, close your eyes, and relax. Take a few peaceful breaths, and then begin to think about one of your greatest passions. It might be an idea, a possession, an activity, or a person. Create a detailed visualization of yourself involved with this passion. As you watch yourself, notice how your body responds. What feelings arise? Where do you feel them? Maybe you notice a tingling or warmth. Maybe you feel a sense of positive energy in part or all of your body. Continue to imagine yourself involved with your passion, and enjoy the feelings that this picture evokes. When you are ready, gently bring your attention back to the present moment, and open your eyes.

When you have finished and while your feelings are still fresh, take a few minutes to write from your heart about what this passion means to you.

_____

_____

_____

_____

_____

_____

today's affirmation

My passions help tell me who I am.

know this

When friends try to talk you into thinking, feeling, or acting a certain way, it's called peer pressure. People do this to feel better about themselves. When people have healthy self-esteem, they don't need to pressure others. When people have healthy self-esteem, they don't need to give in to peer pressure.

When some kids at school learned that Samantha's parents would be away for the weekend, they urged her to have a party. Sam's older sister, Alisha, was supposed to "watch" her, but Alisha would be working the overnight shift at her job.

Sam had never taken advantage of her family and didn't want to lose their trust. But everyone told her she shouldn't worry. They said her parents would never find out.

Sam didn't know what to do. Some of the popular kids who never talked to her were asking her to invite them. As word got around, kids she didn't even know were asking about the party. It felt awesome to have so many people paying attention to her.

Sam talked to her best friends, Jessica and Anna. Jessica said, "Don't let people push you around. Do what you really want to do." That was the problem—Sam really wanted all these kids to keep liking her, and she wanted to keep her parents' trust, too. But everyone kept saying they'd never find out, so maybe it didn't matter. "I'll be your friend either way," said Anna. "Do what you want."

try this

Tell what you think Samantha should do and why.

_____

_____

If Samantha has the party, who will be her friends that night?

_____

_____

If Samantha doesn't have the party, who will be her friends that night?

_____

_____

If Samantha has the party, who will be her friends two weeks afterward?

_____

_____

If Samantha doesn't have the party, who will be her friends two weeks afterward?

_____

_____

Tell who you think has healthy self-esteem in this story and why.

_____

_____

now try this

Circle any of the following that describe things you have felt pressured to do. Check any you have pressured others to do. (You may have both a circle and a check mark for some items.)

gossip	dress a certain way
smoke	like or not like certain people
drink	watch certain shows or movies
join a certain club	take certain classes
do drugs	wear your hair a certain way
steal	listen to particular music
have a certain body size	use sexual behaviors you do not like
follow a particular religion	get tattoos or piercings
play certain sports	use sexual behaviors you are not ready for

Describe one of the situations you circled. How healthy was your self-esteem in this situation?

_____

_____

Describe one of the situations you checked. How healthy was your self-esteem in this situation?

_____

_____

Peer pressure from others works when it feels too hard to stand up for ourselves. Picture yourself in a peer-pressure situation you have actually encountered. Choose the words you could say if it happens again, or write your own.

"No thanks, that's not for me."   "No, thank you."

"No thanks, I'll pass."   "No, I don't do that."

"No, I'd rather not."   "No thanks, not my style."

"No, I don't want to."   "No thanks, I'm not into that."

today's affirmation

I have the strength to stand up to peer pressure; I will decide what's right for me.

know this

When you are struggling to decide how to handle a life challenge, try looking at it from a bigger perspective. Look beyond the personalities and the problem, and ask yourself *Who do I want to be in the universe?* to help make behavior choices that are in line with your authentic self.

When facing a challenging situation you're not sure how to handle, it's easy to get caught up in confusion, frustration, or pain. You may think through option after option, trying to predict what would happen if you acted one way or another. You may try to second-guess what people will think or say in response to your choice. You may spend a lot of time worrying that you'll end up feeling embarrassed or upset.

We get caught up in insecure thinking by letting other people's potential reactions drive our decisions. If we always let what other people think sway us, we'll never have peace of mind. We'll just shift from one side of the fence to the other and back again, trying to do what others want us to.

We can get out of this mess by looking at the situation from a bigger perspective. Instead of asking *What will they think of me?* we ask *Who do I want to be in the universe?*

This question draws our minds to the bigger ideas of who we really are and what we want to contribute to this planet. What kind of person do we want to be? What kind of values do we want to live by? How do we want to relate to others?

Asking this question can help us think more clearly about behavior choices that will keep us true to our authentic selves.

try this

Make a list of people you admire for the way they live their lives. These might be family members, friends, public figures, or people from history. Next to each name, write what quality of that person's character you would like to develop in yourself.

_____

_____

_____

_____

Answer the following:

What do I want to stand for?

_____

What do I want to contribute to the planet?

_____

What would I like to be remembered for?

_____

If you had the power to change the world, tell what it would look like when you were done.

_____

now try this

Think about the kind of person you want to be, and tell how you would act in each of the following situations.

You are with friends at the mall and see a girl walking with a limp. One of your friends starts to walk with a pretend limp, and soon the rest are laughing and doing the same. They want you to join in. The girl looks back, and you see the pain and embarrassment on her face.

_____

_____

_____

_____

A good friend borrows your favorite shirt and gets a huge stain on the front. It won't wash out, and the shirt is ruined.

_____

_____

_____

_____

Your little brother annoys you all the time. You see some bigger kids at the bus stop hassling him and grabbing his backpack.

_____

_____

_____

_____

Your cousin wants you to do his homework for him because he doesn't understand it.
He says it's not really cheating because you go to different schools.

_____

_____

_____

_____

After an argument with your best friend, he refuses to talk to you. All your other
friends say you are in the right.

_____

_____

_____

_____

Now think of a real-life conflict you are having with someone or another situation that
is troubling you. Tell how you could act based on your ideals.

_____

_____

_____

today's affirmation

I choose my actions by thinking about who I want to be in the universe.

know this

Because you are the only person with your specific combination of talents, skills, and gifts, you have a unique contribution to make to the universe. Understanding this concept, exploring it, and staying true to your path will help you live your truth no matter what others may say or do.

When you start listening to the authentic voice within you, you will get a clearer idea about what is best for you and what isn't, including which paths in life are right for you.

These may be daily paths you encounter when deciding whether to play basketball or volleyball, babysit or take a fast-food job, or become friends with one group or another. Or they may be bigger paths that stretch out further into the future, leading to career and life choices. There is no one else exactly like you, so there is no one else whose path is exactly right for you.

No one can fill the very same purpose as another human being. Learning about your unique purpose can give you greater confidence in your value and the special contribution you alone can make to the world. Understanding that purpose, or coming closer to it, can give you something to believe in when you feel uncertain or vulnerable. Knowing without doubt that you are alive for a special reason can give you the strength to remain true to your convictions when others try to persuade you to move away from them.

Important Note: If what you believe to be your purpose might lead you to act in an illegal, immoral, or unethical way, or to do something that will get you in trouble, *check it out*. It is most likely a misguided thought. A true, healthy purpose will rarely lead to a negative consequence.

try this

Great artists, inventors, and people of wisdom have always followed their given purpose to find success. Write the names of real people you know who you think are living their true life purpose, and tell why you think they are.

_____

_____

_____

_____

_____

If you have the chance, talk to these people about their experiences. You might ask them when they first knew their purpose, how it may have changed over time, or the steps they took to pursue it. Record anything they say that is helpful to you.

_____

_____

_____

_____

_____

now try this

You may have a good idea of what your life purpose is, or you may have no idea at all. Either way it's okay. If you keep exploring and accepting your authentic self, you will eventually find your purpose.

Rate each activity listed below on a scale of 1 (low) to 10 (high) according to how appealing it sounds to you. Try to respond from your intuition rather than thinking too much.

_____ swimming with dolphins

_____ caring for people

_____ teaching children

_____ being outdoors

_____ using your mind

_____ sailing a boat

_____ working with technology

_____ leading others

_____ traveling internationally

_____ serving others

_____ maintaining a household

_____ improving health conditions

_____ planning a city

_____ speaking passionately

_____ inspiring people

_____ working at a computer

_____ moving your body

_____ playing with children

_____ working with numbers

_____ writing books

_____ having your own business

_____ playing sports

_____ working with animals

_____ improving the environment

Which activities did you rate higher than 5?

_____

_____

Which did you rate 5 or lower?

_____

_____

Describe any patterns you see in your ratings.

_____

_____

Make a list of your natural talents and gifts.

_____

_____

_____

How do your ratings compare to your talents and gifts?

_____

_____

When you find yourself struggling with self-doubt, or caught up in negative details, ask yourself:

Who am I here to help?

_____

What am I here to do?

_____

What is my purpose today?

_____

today's affirmation

Remembering that I have a unique purpose in life helps me stay true to myself.

the power of attitude 26

know this

Your attitude—the outlook your thoughts create —is literally the most powerful tool you have for making a happy life for yourself. It affects the way you experience *everything*, including yourself.

On a hot, humid day, Sara and Brittney were finishing a marathon. They had been running for hours. Both were feeling the same degree of heat, exhaustion, and thirst; both were dripping with sweat and ready to drop.

As they crossed the finish line, they saw a glass half-filled with water on a table in front of them. Sara looked at the glass from a positive attitude and thought, Fantastic! Water! Just what I need! Should I drink it or pour it over my head? *There was a mile-wide grin on her face. She felt happy, thrilled, fortunate, and relieved.*

Brittney looked at the same glass of water from a negative attitude and thought, Oh no! Only a half glass? I need a million glasses! This is awful! *Brittney's face sank. She felt upset, angry, disappointed, cheated, and afraid.*

The significance of this story is that:

- both girls were in the same condition;

- both girls encountered the same situation;

- both girls had *completely different experiences* of this situation.

What this means is:

- It was not the situation that created their experiences; it was the thoughts generated by their attitudes. Sara's positive attitude generated positive thoughts, producing positive feelings, and she had a positive experience. Brittney's negative attitude generated negative thoughts, producing negative feelings, and she had a negative experience.

- It is our thoughts generated by our attitude that create our feelings and our experience of any situation.

try this

For each situation, identify a feeling that could be created by each different thought. Would this thought/feeling combination create a positive experience or a negative one? Use a check mark.

Shayla studied hard but only got a low C on her math test.

Thought	Feeling	Negative Experience	Positive Experience
I am so stupid! I'll never get into college.			
This teacher is so unfair.			
I didn't even pass the last test, so at least I improved.			

Charlie's younger brother has a learning disability, and their parents spend far more time helping him with homework than they do Charlie.

Thought	Feeling	Negative Experience	Positive Experience
I'm glad Mom and Dad still have time to come to my softball games.			
My brother is such a suck-up.			
They love him more than me.			

Kayla said hi to Rob when she saw him in the hallway, but Rob didn't say hi back.

Thought	Feeling	Negative Experience	Positive Experience
He's so stuck up.			
He might not have heard me because he was talking to Carl.			
He probably thinks I'm an idiot.			

now try this

Briefly describe a situation you are struggling with.

_____

_____

_____

_____

Write two thoughts that would create negative feelings and make this a negative experience.

_____

_____

Write two thoughts that would create positive feelings and make this a more positive experience.

_____

_____

If you have a negative attitude and think negative thoughts about yourself, how will you experience yourself?

_____

_____

_____

If you have a positive attitude and think positive thoughts about yourself, how will you experience yourself?

_____

_____

_____

Who decides what you will think about yourself?

_____

_____

Who controls your self-esteem?

_____

_____

today's affirmation

When I choose a positive attitude and positive thoughts,
I create positive experiences.

27 the power of managing feelings

know this

All feelings are okay. It's what you do with them that will either hurt or help you. When you are aware of your feelings, you can learn to manage them in a healthy way.

Lakeisha couldn't sit still. Her stomach had butterflies, and it was hard to focus in health class. Ms. Elsbury, her health teacher, asked what was wrong. Lakeisha didn't answer, but her eyes filled with tears. She felt embarrassed and looked away.

"What's going on?" Ms. Elsbury asked when they were in her office.

"I don't want to talk about it," said Lakeisha.

"If we don't let feelings out, they actually get bigger," said Ms. Elsbury.

"Well, I don't want that," said Lakeisha. She told Ms. Elsbury that her mom was in the hospital. Her dad visited there every evening, and she was taking care of her younger sisters. Lakeisha was worried about her mom and wasn't able to concentrate or keep up with homework.

"What's the hardest part?" asked Ms. Elsbury.

"I'm afraid my mom won't get better," said Lakeisha. "But if I feel that fear, I might cry and never stop."

"When we're afraid of feelings, we tend to push them away," said Ms. Elsbury. "But they don't go away; they're only hidden temporarily. When they resurface, they're even stronger. Let's look at a plan for managing feelings." Ms. Elsbury gave Lakeisha the following handout and read it with her.

Four-Step Plan for Managing Feelings

1. **Name the feeling.** What is it? Sadness, anger, joy, compassion, disappointment, embarrassment, disgust, shame, love?

2. **Accept the feeling.** It is always okay to feel your feelings. Remind yourself of this. Quietly to yourself or out loud, say: "It's okay to feel _____."

3. **Express the feeling.** Expressing a feeling is the only way to release it. It's important to express it in a way that doesn't hurt you or anyone else. Writing, speaking, physical movement, relaxation, crying, singing, and drawing can all be safe ways to express feelings.

4. **Take care of yourself in a healthy way.** What do you need right now to take care of yourself? A hug, a nap, a shower, a walk, a friend, a party, attention, compassion? You can give yourself whatever you need at the moment.

"I've never thought about what to do with feelings before," said Lakeisha.

"That's okay," said Ms. Elsbury. "It's something you can learn—just like you learned to add and spell and tie your shoes. Managing feelings is one of the most important skills we ever learn. It directly affects our success and happiness in every area of life. When we're confident in managing feelings, we have healthier self-esteem, too."

try this

To become familiar with your feelings, make enough copies of the following chart to last a week. Then start paying attention to your feelings as you go through the days. Record what you observe. The list below may help you identify your feelings. Remember, all feelings are okay, but expressing them should never hurt yourself or others.

abandoned	content	loving	stressed	shocked
guilty	excited	happy	embarrassed	confused
surprised	disappointed	brave	anxious	lonely
irritated	jealous	peaceful	worried	angry
sad	afraid	betrayed	frustrated	apprehensive
thrilled	ashamed	relieved	relaxed	depressed

Day _____	What I feel	Where I notice it in my body	How I express it
Morning			
Afternoon			
Night			

now try this

When you consciously manipulate, or do something with, your feelings, you are taking charge of them. Try any or all of the following ways to work with your feelings. Use the blank lines to add your own ideas. Give yourself some time to complete this.

After identifying your feeling:

_____ Say your feeling out loud: "I am feeling _____ right now."

_____ Write a paragraph or more about it.

_____ Describe it to someone you trust.

_____ Express it on paper without words, using color, line, texture, or form.

_____ If it fits with your feeling, cry it out.

_____ Write a letter to someone you are having feelings about. Do not send the letter.

_____ Write or draw your feeling and put the paper through a shredder.

_____ Write or draw your feeling and frame the paper.

_____ Write or draw your feeling and give the paper away to someone else.

_____ Write or draw your feeling and tear up the paper.

_____ Write or draw your feeling and crumple the paper up and throw it away.

_____ Write or draw your feeling on bathroom tissue and flush it away.

_____ Do some safe physical exercise—such as walking, swimming, or stretching—to release the energy of your feeling.

_____ Sing your feeling.

_____ Play out your feeling on an instrument.

_____ _____

_____ _____

After you try each activity, rate how well it worked for you (1 = ineffective, 10 = very effective.) Write your rating number next to the description of the activity.

today's affirmation

All my feelings are okay; I manage them in a healthy way.

know this

If you view discomfort as a negative, you will try to avoid it and will lose its potential benefits. If you see it in a positive light, you can transcend it and use it as a powerful tool to develop self-awareness and inner strength and reach your goals.

Morgan felt discomfort because everyone else had dressed up for Tony's party and she was wearing cut-off jeans. She was tempted to sneak out the back door, but she didn't really want to; she had been looking forward to the party for weeks. Morgan realized that her discomfort was about a fear of being rejected or made fun of. She decided to remember that it didn't matter what she wore—her real friends wouldn't care. A couple of kids teased her in a friendly way, and she laughed with them about it, but by the end of the night, she'd proved herself right—her real friends didn't care. She felt good about herself for tolerating her discomfort.

Matt felt discomfort at the football tryouts because it seemed everyone else was so much better than him. He changed his mind about trying out and rode home on the late bus. He went to his room and tried to do homework, but he kept thinking about how much he'd wanted to make the team, and how embarrassed he would feel when people asked him what happened. Matt felt his self-esteem take a nosedive.

Vicki felt discomfort about trusting Shawna when they became friends. Vicki had been hurt before when friends betrayed her. She told herself she wouldn't become close with anyone again. But Shawna was so nice; they had a lot in common and had so much fun together. Part of Vicki wanted to stop seeing Shawna so the discomfort would go away and she would feel safe again. Part of her wanted to tolerate the discomfort and hope that Shawna wouldn't betray her. She didn't know what to do.

David won a free concert ticket because he was the thirtieth caller on a radio program. When he picked up his ticket, he found out he could get a second free ticket, but he'd have to stand in a long line that would take about an hour. David wanted the second ticket so he could take a friend to the concert, but he would feel discomfort standing in a boring line for so long with people he didn't know. He couldn't decide if he should stay or go.

try this

Circle the word or phrase that best describes how high your discomfort would have been if you were in Morgan's situation. Then tell what you would have done in her place.

very low   low   medium   high   very high

_____

_____

Circle the word or phrase that best describes how high your discomfort would have been if you were in Matt's situation. Then tell what you would have done in his place.

very low   low   medium   high   very high

_____

_____

Circle the word or phrase that best describes how high your discomfort would be if you were in Vicki's situation. Then describe what Vicki might gain if she tolerates the discomfort of not knowing if she will be hurt by Shawna.

very low   low   medium   high   very high

_____

_____

Circle the word or phrase that best describes how high your discomfort would be if you were in David's situation. Then describe what David might gain if he tolerates the discomfort of waiting in line.

very low   low   medium   high   very high

_____

_____

now try this

Write a number from 1 (low) to 10 (high) next to each description to tell how strong your discomfort would be in this situation. Then describe what you might gain from tolerating the discomfort.

_____ You are lifting weights to gain muscle strength, and you're bored only halfway through the workout.

Benefit of tolerating the discomfort of continuing: _____

_____

_____ You're babysitting for neighbors, and they call to ask if you can stay two extra hours. They pay well and you need the money, but you're already eager to leave and meet your friends.

Benefit of tolerating the discomfort of staying: _____

_____

_____ Your date, who has so far been fun and nice and interesting, suggests watching a TV show you can't stand.

Benefit of tolerating the discomfort of watching: _____

_____

_____ You are home on a Friday night and feeling lonely. Some kids call and ask you to do something that would be fun, but that you could get in trouble for.

Benefit of tolerating the discomfort of loneliness: _____

_____

_____ Your parents are fighting again, and you're feeling depressed. You've thought about running away before, and tonight it feels like it might be the only answer.

Benefit of tolerating the discomfort of staying: _____

_____

_____ You need to retake a class you failed in order to graduate. You hate the subject and don't get along with the teacher.

Benefit of tolerating the discomfort of retaking the class: _____

_____

Circle the situations in which you ever tolerated discomfort and gained something. Then write your own story of a time this happened.

learned to walk	went to the dentist
woke up earlier than you'd like	did a boring task
talked to someone new	admitted you were wrong
studied for a test	helped a person in need
asked for help	tried a new activity
got a vaccination	faced a fear

My story:

_____

_____

_____

_____

_____

Describe a challenge in your life now where you must decide whether or not you will tolerate discomfort. Tell what the benefits of tolerating the discomfort would be.

_____

_____

_____

_____

_____

today's affirmation

I can tolerate discomfort and gain something from doing so.

the power of responsibility

know this

Blaming other people or external circumstances for what your life is like gives away your power and leads to negativity and helplessness. Accepting responsibility for your life means you are in charge of your thoughts, feelings, and actions. It gives you back your power and lets you grow into your authentic self.

Mr. Jordan, Connor's English teacher, asked Connor to stay after class. Connor had always been a good writer and an A student in English, but his last few papers had been late, and he had stopped participating in class—when he bothered to show up. Mr. Jordan asked whether anything was wrong.

"A lot," said Connor. "I didn't make the basketball team because the coach is way too picky about skills. And my mom is marrying this guy I hardly know. I'm feeling really angry at these people for ruining my life, and now they're ruining my grades, too."

"Those things sound hard," said Mr. Jordan. "I don't blame you for feeling upset. But it sounds like you're blaming other people for your lack of happiness and success."

"Well, it is their fault," said Connor. "If the coach were more reasonable, I would have made the team. If my mom weren't doing something stupid, I could concentrate more on school."

"When we don't like something about our life," said Mr. Jordan, "it might feel easier to blame someone else. Then we don't have to do anything to change. But blaming makes us powerless victims. It also creates unhealthy self-esteem, because deep down inside we know our happiness is our job, not someone else's."

"But Coach and Mom aren't going to change their minds—and what they're doing affects me a lot. I am powerless over them!" said Connor.

"So take back your power," said Mr. Jordan. "Ask the coach what you can do differently to make the team next year, and then improve and show him what you can do. Let your mother know how you feel, and then decide you're not going to let her choices affect your happiness. Take responsibility for your own actions and feelings. Blaming leads to negativity and helplessness. Taking responsibility lets you grow into your authentic self and your true potential."

try this

Gretchen was caught smoking cigarettes and was suspended from school. She blamed her older brother because he had given her the cigarettes.

How could Gretchen take back her power? _____

_____

Scott failed his history test. He blamed the teacher because she hadn't given the class a study guide.

How could Scott take back his power? _____

_____

Paige got home late three nights in a row for her 10:00 p.m. curfew. She blamed her parents because the curfew was too early.

How could Paige take back her power? _____

_____

Joe was mad at Ethan for sharing a secret that Joe told him not to share. Ethan blamed Joe for telling him the secret in the first place.

How could Ethan take back his power? _____

_____

Laura has low self-esteem. She blames her parents for being too critical.

How could Laura take back her power? _____

_____

now try this

Put a B next to any situations that describe times you feel like blaming someone else for your actions.

_____ I stub my toe.

_____ I drop my books.

_____ I trip on the sidewalk or in the hall.

_____ I receive a low grade on a test or paper.

_____ I spill my drink.

_____ I get in trouble for arguing with my sibling.

_____ I feel angry.

_____ I bump into someone.

_____ I forget to do my chores.

_____ I sleep through my alarm.

_____ I miss the ball in a sports competition.

_____ I forget my homework.

_____ I lose my homework.

_____ My bedroom is messy.

_____ I accidentally break a window, lamp, or other property.

_____ I am late for class.

_____ I go over the limit on my cell phone minutes.

Circle anything that is your responsibility. Add more of your own.

my feelings	my actions	how I feel about myself
my job	my beliefs	how I treat other people
how I treat myself	my chores	my schoolwork
_____	_____	_____

Name the people you tend to blame for your unhappiness.

At home:

_____

_____

At school:

_____

_____

With friends:

_____

_____

You may have learned where your unhealthy self-esteem came from. This is understanding, not blaming. Once you understand, it is your job to do the repair work. Describe what you can do to take responsibility for creating healthier self-esteem.

_____

_____

_____

What thoughts do you need to change?

_____

_____

_____

What behaviors do you need to change?

_____

_____

_____

On a separate sheet of paper, write a letter to someone you have blamed. Tell that person you are taking back your power. (Decide whether or not you will really send this letter.)

today's affirmation

I keep my power by taking responsibility for my actions.

30 the power of intuition

know this

Discovering and listening to your intuition or "inner voice" can lead you to your authentic self and the path that is right for you. When you learn to trust your authentic self, you can better know and follow your true path.

Sometimes we have a strong, deep feeling about what is right for us. Maybe we've always wanted to teach, practice medicine, or climb mountains. Maybe we are drawn to a particular sport or hobby. When we think about it, we may not know exactly why we want to do this; we just know it is a deep yearning, and when we participate in this activity, it feels good.

Sometimes we have a strong, deep feeling about making a decision—we just know that one decision is right and another is not. We may also have a strong, deep feeling that something is going to happen. We might think *I have a feeling Mariah will call soon,* or *I have a feeling I'll be back here.*

This strong, deep feeling is called intuition. The messages from intuition are both felt in our bodies and heard in our minds. Sometimes these messages are not in agreement with logic. Sometimes we don't listen to them and then we think, *I knew I shouldn't have done that—why didn't I listen to my intuition?*

Paying attention to our intuitive messages can help find our authentic selves. Staying true to those selves can help us build and maintain healthy self-esteem.

try this

Without thinking—just using your "gut feeling" or intuition—circle the answers that are right for you.

Which color appeals to you most?

red   orange   yellow   blue   green   purple   brown   black   white

Which shape or line appeals to you most?

Which number appeals to you most?

6   3   10   2   5   8   4   9   7   1

Which symbol appeals to you most?

Which font appeals to you most?

this one   this one   this one   this one   THIS ONE

Name any people you feel you just click with or connect with in an unexplainable way.

_____

_____

_____

Some people experience a deep knowing that they want to be an architect or a parent or to travel or study art. Describe any deep knowings you have about your future.

_____

_____

_____

Describe any time you may have "felt" an answer in your body. Maybe it was a tightening in your chest or a quickening of your heartbeat.

_____

_____

_____

Describe any time you felt yourself drawn to something or someone, as if there was a magnetic pull between you.

_____

_____

_____

Describe any other time in your life when you noticed your intuition speaking to you.

_____

_____

_____

now try this

For the next few days, pay attention to and record any hunches you have. Hunches don't always follow logic. They are thoughts or feelings that you sense rather than know intellectually. For example, *I have a feeling it's going to rain,* or *I have a feeling we'll win although the odds are with the other team.*

Important Note: If your intuition ever tells you to do something that is illegal, immoral, unethical, or will get you into trouble, *check it out*. It is most likely a misguided thought, as real intuition will rarely lead to a negative consequence.

Day 1 hunches: _____

_____

Day 2 hunches: _____

_____

Day 3 hunches: _____

_____

To practice moving past your intellect and listening internally, try these exercises. When you are done, describe what each activity was like for you.

- Sit quietly and comfortably with several sheets of blank paper or your computer. Clear your mind, and write, "I remember . . ." Follow with any thoughts that come. Continue writing anything that arises, without thinking about it or judging. Ignore spelling, grammar, punctuation, and any other writing rules you've learned. Simply let your intuitive mind take over and express whatever comes up. Write for as long as you feel comfortable.

  _____

  _____

- Sit quietly and comfortably, and close your eyes. Take a few relaxing breaths, and watch as a scene unfolds in your mind. Let your imagination lead you wherever it will. What do you notice about what appears to you?

125

_____

_____

• At any time during the day, stop your activity for a moment and tune in to yourself. Feel your heartbeat and your breath. Notice what your muscles are doing and let them relax. Close your eyes and feel the energy that animates you. When you have tuned yourself inward, simply listen. Pay attention to any inner messages you get.

_____

_____

• Pay attention to how you respond to people and situations. When you find yourself clinging to rigid thinking, try to let go and open your mind. Let answers and actions come to you from your intuition rather than always filling them in from your brain. Notice how this affects you.

_____

_____

• When it is safe and healthy to do so, make choices that bring you joy. The feeling of joy is deeper and more all-encompassing than happiness. Feeling true joy is usually a signal that we are following our intuition and being true to our authentic selves.

_____

_____

today's affirmation

My intuition is a message from my authentic self.

know this

Gratitude is an attitude of thankfulness and appreciation. When we practice an attitude of gratitude, we give attention to and celebrate all that is good in our life. This raises our level of happiness and peace, both about our circumstances and about ourselves.

Troy felt like he was stuck in a rut. He hated getting out of bed in the morning to hear his parents nagging him to do his chores. He hated sitting through classes, listening to boring teachers. He hated going to work after school, stocking shelves and having to be nice to customers he didn't even know. He hated sitting in his room at night, pretending to do homework he didn't care about. The only time Troy felt happy was when he was with his girlfriend, Carly. But lately even Carly couldn't get him out of his bad mood.

"I'm getting tired of this," Carly told him. "All you do is talk about what's bad. I don't want to hear any more about your awful parents, your awful classes, or your awful job. Your life isn't that terrible, Troy. You just don't appreciate what you've got. And I don't think you appreciate me anymore, either. Maybe we shouldn't hang out together so much."

"Wait," said Troy. "I'm sorry I'm so down. I just can't find any reason to feel happy. I don't want to lose you, but I don't know how to change my life."

"You don't have to change your life," said Carly. "You just have to change your attitude. Instead of complaining, start being grateful. Focus on the good. Be glad you even have parents—you could be an orphan. Be glad you're healthy and can go to school—there's a kid in a hospital somewhere right now who would give anything to sit in one of your boring classes. Be glad you have a job so you can put gas in your car and go to the mall and the movies!"

"You're right," said Troy. "When you put it like that, I realize I do have a lot to be grateful for. I wish I could keep that attitude."

"Just continue to focus on all the good in your life," said Carly. "You'll feel happier, and you'll be a lot nicer to be around."

try this

Like Troy, many of us take a lot for granted. We forget about what we are fortunate to have. There are many people who don't have the things listed below. Think about what it would be like without any of these, and circle those you are grateful for.

sense of sight	place to live	food in the refrigerator
friends	sense of hearing	bed to sleep in
ability to speak	freedom of speech	sense of taste
family	ability to read	education
functioning brain	ability to love	ability to breathe on your own

Finish the following sentences:

I am grateful for _____

_____

I feel lucky because _____

_____

One thing I really appreciate is _____

_____

Something I will always be thankful for is _____

_____

Try to identify and be grateful for the good in you. Tell three things you are grateful for about yourself in each of the following categories.

Physical

1. _____

2. _____

3. _____

Mental

1. _____

2. _____

3. _____

Spiritual

1. _____

2. _____

3. _____

now try this

For the next week, pay attention to the good in your life. Every night before you go to sleep, write down five things you were grateful for that day. These could be anything from "I was able to get out of bed," to "I won the track relay," to "It was a sunny day." Continue to think of more as you fall asleep.

Day 1

1. _____

2. _____

3. _____

4. _____

5. _____

Day 2

1. _____

2. _____

3. _____

4. _____

5. _____

Day 3

1. _____

2. _____

3. _____

4. _____

5. _____

Day 4

1. _____

2. _____

3. _____

4. _____

5. _____

Day 5

1. _____

2. _____

3. _____

4. _____

5. _____

Day 6

1. _____

2. _____

3. _____

4. _____

5. _____

Day 7

1. _____

2. _____

3. _____

4. _____

5. _____

At the end of the week, describe how focusing on the good in your life affected you.

_____

_____

_____

today's affirmation

I focus on all the good in my life.

the power of compassion

---

know this

Compassion means a deep sympathy or caring. Being able to feel compassion for every human being, including yourself, is a cornerstone of healthy self-esteem.

We have all been born, and we all will die. We all want to succeed, and we all want to feel happy. We all want to feel good about ourselves, and we all want to feel loved. We all struggle to survive in a way that will bring us the most peace and the least pain. We are all doing the best we can with what we have.

On the most basic level, everyone is made from the same essential stuff—physically, emotionally, and spiritually. We are all in this life experience together, on an even playing field. No one is greater than—or less than—anyone else
. Realizing the ways we are alike and the basic drives and instincts we all share brings us the gift of compassion.

Compassion arises when we no longer feel insecure about ourselves. We can feel compassion for others when we no longer feel threatened by them. We can feel compassion for ourselves when we accept our human condition—our strengths and our flaws—and when we love and accept ourselves no matter what. Compassion for every living creature helps us achieve healthy self-esteem.

try this

Record the level of concern or sympathy you would feel for each of the following people or animals on a scale of 1 (low) to 10 (high), and then record the feeling or feelings you experience. Choose your feelings from the following list or write your own.

pain   sadness   helplessness   anger

1. your friend whose parent has died

Concern/sympathy: _____   Feeling(s): _____

2. a puppy limping in the street in the rain

Concern/sympathy: _____   Feeling(s): _____

3. a person on the news who lost everything in a hurricane

Concern/sympathy: _____   Feeling(s): _____

4. a child who has a terminal illness

Concern/sympathy: _____   Feeling(s): _____

5. your grandparent who is aging

Concern/sympathy: _____   Feeling(s): _____

6. your younger sibling who was harshly punished by your parents

Concern/sympathy: _____   Feeling(s): _____

7. a blind kitten

Concern/sympathy: _____   Feeling(s): _____

8. a homeless person you see on the street

Concern/sympathy: _____   Feeling(s): _____

9. someone on the side of the highway whose car has broken down

Concern/sympathy: _____   Feeling(s): _____

10. farm animals who are physically abused

Concern/sympathy: _____   Feeling(s): _____

Check any of the following statements you might use when you are speaking with compassion.

☐ "I'm sorry this happened to you."   ☐ "It will be okay."

☐ "How can I help?"   ☐ "I will help you through this."

☐ "Are you okay?"   ☐ "I care about you."

☐ "Tell me what I can do."   ☐ "It will get better."

☐ "I want to help."   ☐ Other: _____

Circle any of these compassionate actions you are comfortable doing:

Listening   Paying attention   Giving financial support

Hugging   Giving time   Other: _____

Giving energy   Giving emotional support

Choose two of the above situations and tell how you would treat that person or animal with compassion.

Number _____

What I would say: _____

What I would do: _____

Number _____

What I would say: _____

What I would do: _____

now try this

What are your thoughts and feelings about treating yourself with compassion?

_____

_____

_____

You may not be used to directing compassion toward yourself, but if you know how to treat others with compassion, you also know how to treat yourself. Think about the compassionate words and actions listed above, and describe how you could show compassion for yourself in the following situations.

Someone turns you down for a date.

_____

_____

You forget the words to your oral presentation.

_____

_____

You don't make the team.

_____

_____

You feel lonely.

_____

_____

You give the wrong answer when the teacher calls on you.

_____

_____

You've had a rough day.

_____

_____

Think of a struggle you've been experiencing recently. On a separate sheet of paper, write a compassionate letter to yourself with regard to this. Use words and feelings you might use to show compassion to your best friend.

today's affirmation

Treating myself with compassion is an act of healthy self-esteem.

33 the power of possibility

know this

Your life is limited only by your thoughts. When you can see the infinite possibilities present in every moment, situation, and person, you have the ability to grow, change, and become anything you desire.

Josh was fishing with his uncle Brian. The conversation turned to the family business, and Josh complained that his dad expected him to join the business some day, but he had no interest in it. He also had no interest in his classes, his after-school job, or being on the basketball team. He felt trapped in his life and sometimes felt like running away.

Uncle Brian asked why Josh didn't make some changes. "That's impossible," Josh said. "Dad expects me to go into the business because I'm the oldest. I have to take certain classes to get into college—except I'd rather go to the police academy. I have to work at a fast-food job because I don't have any other experience. And I can't quit basketball because I've played since grade school."

"That's a lot of 'have-tos' and 'can'ts,'" said Uncle Brian. "It seems you're seeing life from a very narrow perspective. That's really limiting."

"What do you mean?" asked Josh. "How could I see it differently?"

"Instead of seeing traps, see possibilities," said Uncle Brian. "Talk to your dad, and explain what you'd really like to do with your future. Change your classes and get on a track to prepare for police work. Apply for new jobs and see what happens. Try a new sport—or take a break from sports for a while."

"But I feel stuck," said Josh. "Nothing will ever change."

"You're stuck only in your thinking," said Uncle Brian. "The truth is that each moment offers infinite possibilities. We decided to fish today, but that could change at any time. We could decide to go home right now, or we could lie down on the pier and nap. I could push you into the water and jump in after you, and we could both go swimming.

"It might feel like you're trapped by your family, your experiences, or your personality—but in reality, you're trapped only by your thoughts. If you believe you have choices, you'll begin to see them. When we open our minds to infinite possibilities, we can expand and grow, and choose any path we want from the millions before us."

try this

List ten things you do in an average day. After each, list another choice you could make. It doesn't have to be something you would actually do, but open your mind to new possibilities. For example, if you usually get out of bed on the right side, you could exit at the foot. If you usually say "hi," you could say "hey" or "hello." Let your mind practice thinking differently.

Regular Activity

1. _____
2. _____
3. _____
4. _____
5. _____
6. _____
7. _____
8. _____
9. _____
10. _____

Alternate Choice

1. _____
2. _____
3. _____
4. _____
5. _____
6. _____
7. _____
8. _____
9. _____
10. _____

Circle one or more thoughts you feel trapped in from the list below or write your own. Then open your mind, and write a different thought you could choose instead.

"I'm a loser." _____

"I can't change." _____

"I'm bad." _____

"I'm stupid." _____

"I can't do anything right." _____

"I'll never be good enough." _____

Other: _____

_____

_____

now try this

Opening your mind is like opening a door. The wider you open it, the more you see.

Stand at the door of the room you are in now. Open the door one inch, just enough to see past it. List the items you see in the space beyond.

_____

Open the door six inches. Count how many more items you can see.

_____

Open the door three feet. Count how many more items you can see.

_____

Make a list of situations you feel trapped in.

_____

_____

_____

Choose one item from your list and describe it from a trapped perspective—with the door of your mind open only an inch.

_____

_____

_____

Open the door of your mind six inches. Describe the new possibilities you see.

_____

_____

_____

Open the door of your mind three feet. Describe the possibilities you see now.

_____

_____

_____

If possibilities were limitless, what would you do differently tomorrow?

_____

_____

_____

Next week?

_____

_____

_____

Next year?

_____

_____

_____

If possibilities were limitless, how would you choose to think about yourself?

_____

_____

_____

today's affirmation

I can choose from limitless possibilities at every moment.

---

know this

Thoughts are always the beginning steps toward making something happen. When we realize the power of our thoughts, we can use them to help create the life we want.

Everything you do or have ever done began with a thought. If you watch a movie, it's because you first had the thought to do it. If you are wearing clothes, it's because you first had the thought to put them on. If you are in a relationship with someone, it's because you first had the thought to talk to that person.

We usually have a thought of desire first (*I'd like a pizza*), followed by a thought of intention (*I'm going to make a pizza*), and then comes action (getting a pizza from the freezer and putting it in the oven). Sometimes we have thoughts of desire and intention but don't achieve our goal because we don't take action—getting off the couch to make the pizza!

Sometimes you may feel as if you have no power. You may feel hopeless or believe you will never achieve what you want. You may feel as if your life is just "bad" and there is nothing you can do about it. You may think you can't change your self-esteem—it's been unhealthy for too long.

It's true that we don't have control over many things in life. People die, get divorced, betray us, reject us, and hurt us. Situations occur that are difficult or destructive, situations we didn't ask for.

However, no matter what else is happening that we can't control, we can always take control where we do have it. We can follow a desire with an intention and then take action. We can choose intentions and actions that will lead to achieving our goals.

try this

This path illustrates the combination of steps we take from a thought to its outcome. It begins with a thought of desire: *I wish I could ski.* Next comes a thought of intention: *I think I'll take skiing lessons.* Then comes one or more action steps: getting a permission slip signed, taking lessons. And finally, the outcome: skiing down the slopes.

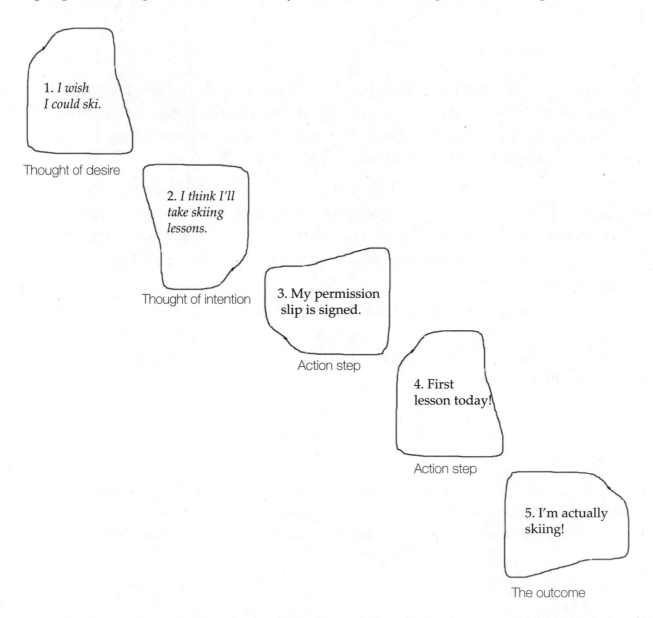

1. *I wish I could ski.*

Thought of desire

2. *I think I'll take skiing lessons.*

Thought of intention

3. My permission slip is signed.

Action step

4. First lesson today!

Action step

5. I'm actually skiing!

The outcome

Write the path for each outcome listed. Often more than two action steps are necessary, but for this activity record only two.

Two friends get tickets to see a very popular band.

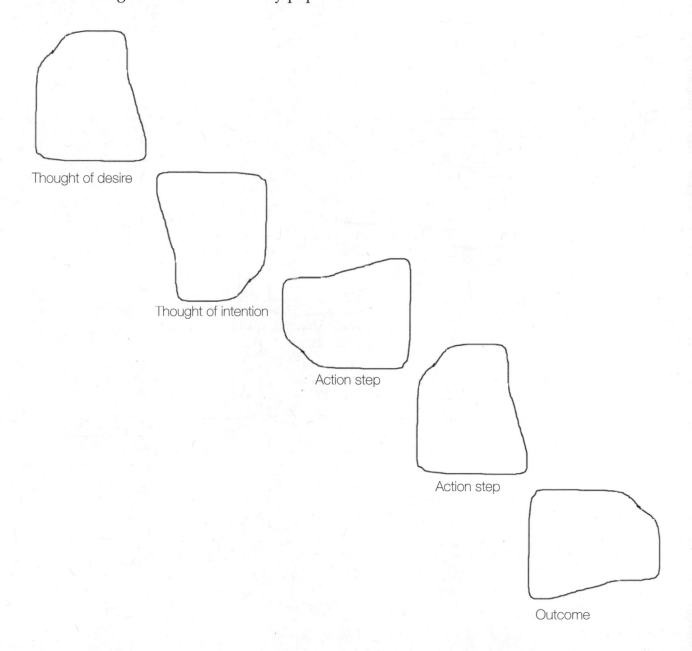

Thought of desire

Thought of intention

Action step

Action step

Outcome

Someone purchases new clothes.

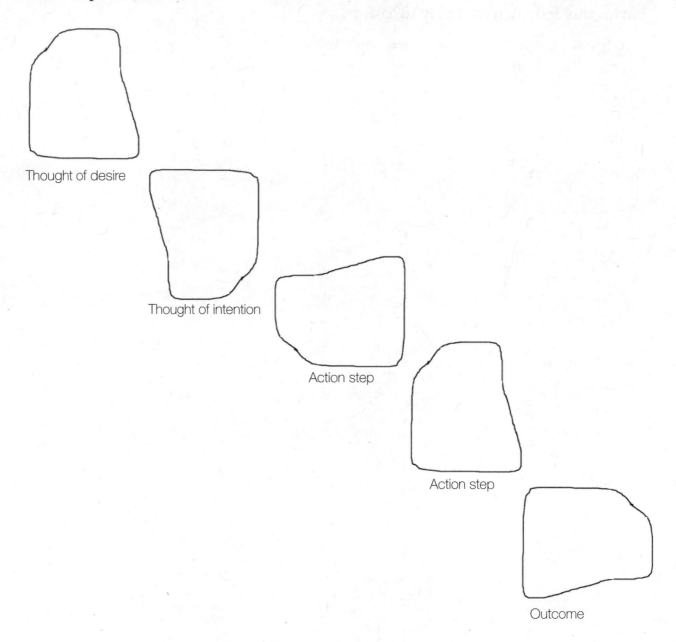

Thought of desire

Thought of intention

Action step

Action step

Outcome

A programmer creates a computer game.

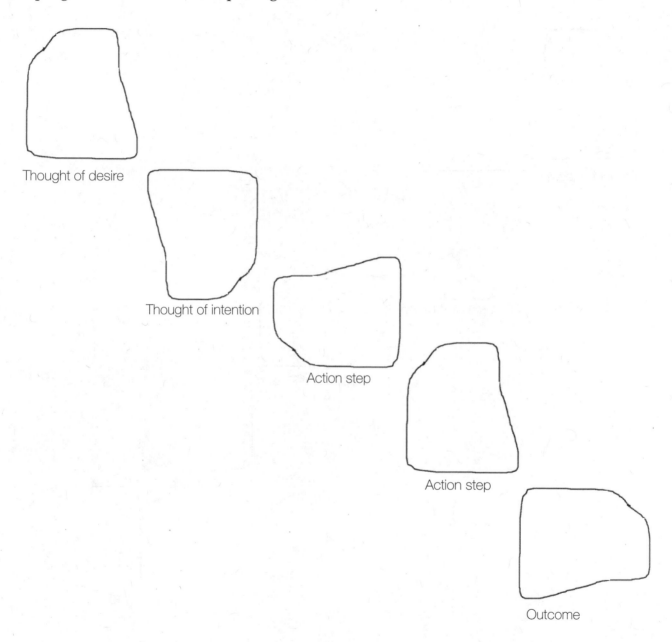

Thought of desire

Thought of intention

Action step

Action step

Outcome

A newly-elected president is being sworn into office.

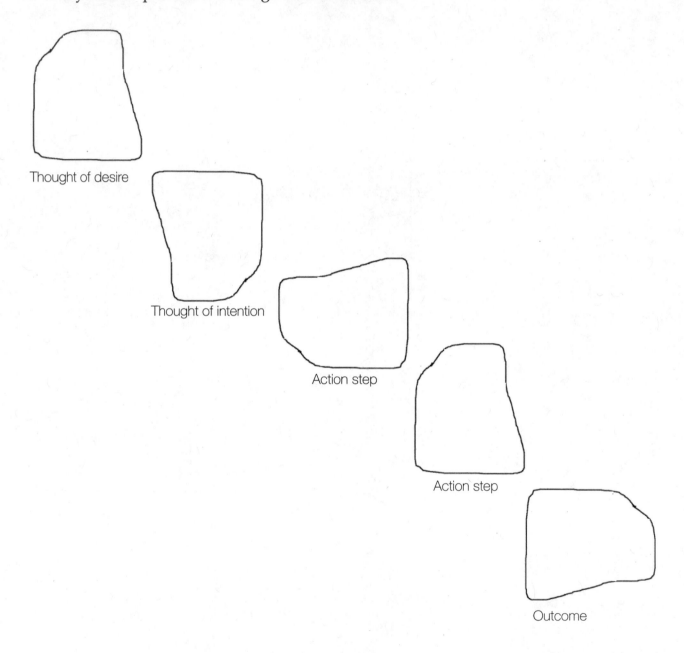

Thought of desire

Thought of intention

Action step

Action step

Outcome

now try this

List five things you have done in your life that began with a thought. These can be anything from learning to walk to going bowling to winning an award.

1. _____

2. _____

3. _____

4. _____

5. _____

List five things you did this morning that began with a thought.

1. _____

2. _____

3. _____

4. _____

5. _____

Write a path for something you would like to happen in your life.

Thought of desire: _____

_____

Thought of intention: _____

_____

Action step(s): _____

_____

Outcome: _____

Write a path for achieving healthier self-esteem for yourself.

Thought of desire: _____

_____

Thought of intention: _____

_____

Action step(s): _____

_____

Outcome: _____

today's affirmation

I achieve my goals by beginning with my thoughts.

the power of conviction

---

know this

Conviction is a strong belief and certitude. When you believe deeply in yourself and your goals, you gain the strength to get through challenges, to follow your dreams, and to remain true to yourself.

Bethany had been through a lot. She was born with a number of heart problems that required multiple surgeries before she was five and prevented her from participating in many activities. Her father had walked out when things got too hard, and her mother took a second job to support Bethany and her sister, Tia. Bethany and Tia were often alone after school because their mom couldn't afford day care or a babysitter. On those afternoons, they would video chat with Grandma Jen, who would help them with homework, encourage them, share her wisdom, or sometimes just tell funny stories to make them laugh.

Grandma Jen had experienced a lot in her own life. She dropped out of eighth grade to take care of her younger sisters after her mother was killed in an accident. Once her sisters were grown, she finally got her high school certificate and met Grandpa Johnny. They had two children before he was drafted into the military. The war depressed Johnny, and he turned to alcohol to cope. When he came home, Grandma Jen stood by him as he went through treatment and recovery from addiction.

"There will always be challenges in life," Grandma Jen would tell Bethany and Tia. "Since we can't get rid of them, we have to learn how to handle them. One of the most important things you can do when times get hard is never give up! You might have challenges with friends, school, health, or family all at once. You might feel like people have pushed you down and each time you try to stand up they push you down again. But if you have the conviction that you can make it, you can."

try this

Imagine that the outline of the body in this frame represents you. Fill it in or decorate it to show yourself filled with strength and conviction. Use colors, lines, forms, or textures that depict an unwavering belief in yourself.

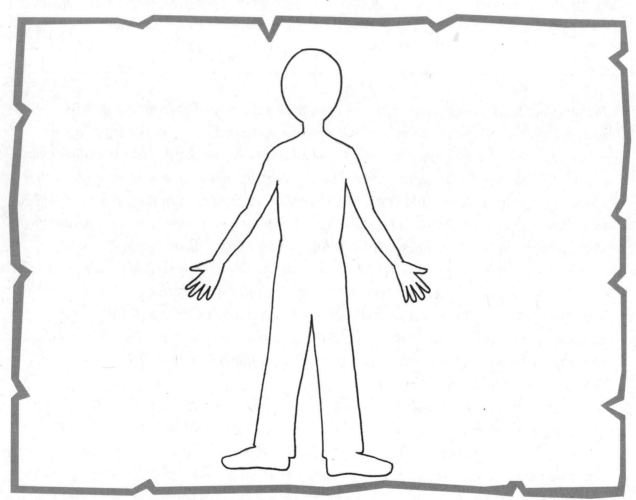

Around the picture, write statements of conviction. Choose from these suggestions or write your own.

"I believe in myself."   "I believe in positive outcomes."

"I refuse to be discouraged."   "I believe good is coming my way."

"I will not give up."

now try this

List anything you have accomplished in your life. These achievements may be mental, physical, or spiritual; they could relate to family, friends, school, or activities. Put a star next to those that were the hardest to attain. Tell how your life would have been different if you had given up before you achieved these goals.

_____

_____

_____

_____

_____

Choose one of the items you starred to use in the picture below. Write your accomplishment on the line under the picture. Draw yourself at the start of the obstacle course. Write or draw your accomplishment at the end of the course. At each obstacle, write or draw something you had to overcome to reach your goal. (For example, if your accomplishment was passing an English class, your obstacles might have been tests, papers, or a teacher who was a hard grader.)

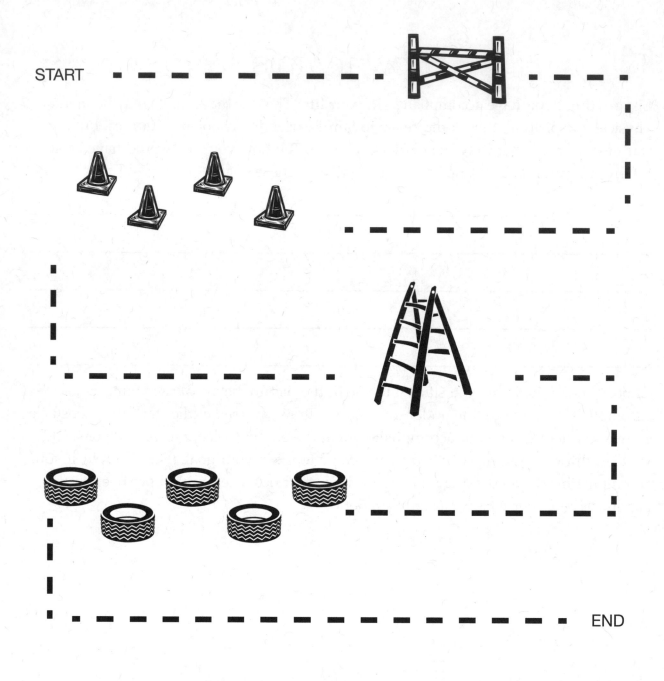

Title the bottom of the next picture with the name of a current challenge you are facing. Draw yourself at the start of the obstacle course. Write or draw your goal at the end of the course. At each obstacle, write or draw something that might make it hard for you to reach your goal.

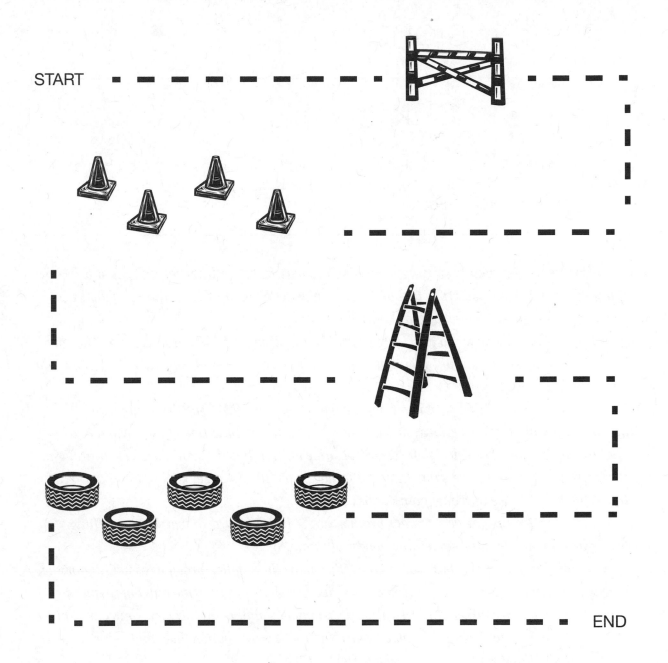

START

END

---

today's affirmation

I refuse to give up! I refuse to be discouraged!

36 the power of positive decisions

know this

Positive decisions are those that are most likely to result in positive outcomes. When you make a positive decision, even if it is not the easiest one to follow through on, you create a better chance of having a positive outcome.

Jemal's little brother had been caught copying a report from the Internet instead of writing it himself. He was also starting to hang around kids who had a bad reputation. Jemal was concerned and asked him what was going on.

"It was so much easier to copy that paper than do it myself," his brother said. "I'm not good at writing. And I know I might get into trouble with those kids, but it's fun to do risky stuff—it feels cool."

"It might have seemed easier to copy the paper," Jemal said, "but then look what happened—you were suspended for a day and had to rewrite the report, and Mom and Dad grounded you. Your decision seemed positive at first, but it wasn't, because it brought a negative outcome. It's the same thing with those kids. It might feel cool to hang out with them, but what is the outcome going to be?"

"I know it'll be negative," Jemal's brother said. "But it's hard to wait for something better when you can have something good right now."

"I know," said Jemal, "but would you rather have the smaller problem of waiting or the bigger problem of the negative outcome? Positive decisions get positive outcomes, and you can feel good about yourself, too. Negative decisions not only bring negative outcomes, but also make you end up feeling bad about yourself. You deserve better than that—think about making choices that will make your life better, not worse."

try this

For each situation, write one possible positive decision and one possible negative decision and tell what the outcome would be for each.

Julia is buying only one candy bar, but she has to stand in a long line to pay for it. She doesn't have much time. She thinks about just putting it in her pocket and walking out.

Possible positive decision: _____

_____

Outcome: _____

_____

Possible negative decision: _____

_____

Outcome: _____

_____

Patrick always wishes that Evan would talk to him because Evan is really popular. One day Evan asks Patrick to cheat for him on an upcoming test.

Possible positive decision: _____

_____

Outcome: _____

_____

Possible negative decision: _____

_____

Outcome: _____

_____

Sophia's boyfriend wants her to be more physically intimate than she wants to be. She's afraid he might break up with her if she doesn't agree.

Possible positive decision: _____

_____

Outcome: _____

_____

Possible negative decision: _____

_____

Outcome: _____

_____

Tony learns some personal information about a student no one likes. He knows that sharing the information would make him look cool.

Possible positive decision: _____

_____

Outcome: _____

_____

Possible negative decision: _____

_____

Outcome: _____

_____

Cassie's uncle is in the hospital with a terminal illness. She was planning to go with her family to visit him. Then she was invited to the best party of the year on the same day.

Possible positive decision: _____

_____

Outcome: _____

_____

Possible negative decision: _____

_____

Outcome: _____

_____

now try this

Observe and record decisions you or others make throughout the day. Next to each, circle the plus sign if you think it is a positive decision and the minus sign if you think it is a negative decision, and tell why.

+ − 1. _____

_____

Because: _____

_____

+ − 2. _____

_____

Because: _____

_____

+ − 3. _____

_____

Because: _____

_____

+ – 4. _____

_____

Because: _____

_____

+ – 5. _____

_____

Because: _____

_____

Explain a positive decision you once made and describe its outcome.

_____

_____

_____

How was your self-esteem affected by this outcome?

_____

_____

_____

Explain a negative decision you once made and describe its outcome.

_____

_____

_____

How was your self-esteem affected by this outcome?

_____

_____

_____

Imagine and describe a world where everyone made only positive decisions. What would be different or the same?

_____

_____

_____

today's affirmation

Making positive decisions will bring me positive outcomes.

the power of facing
challenges head on 37

know this

When a situation looks difficult, you might want to ignore it, avoid it, or make it go away. But when we don't face challenges head on, we end up making things worse. Facing challenges helps us feel better about ourselves and creates healthy self-esteem.

Ellen was given a detention slip for getting to class late. She was supposed to take it home, have it signed by her parents, and then stay an hour after school on Friday. Ellen knew her parents would ground her. They'd been on her for everything lately, and this was going to make things worse. As she was walking to the bus, the detention slip fell out of her books and onto the ground. Ellen hesitated. Instead of picking it up, she watched the wind whisk it away. Ellen smiled. **That takes care of that problem,** *she thought.*

On Monday morning, Ellen's father got a call from the vice principal. Ellen now had a second detention for not showing up for the first. One more and she could be suspended. Ellen's parents grounded her for two weeks—one for getting a detention in the first place, the second for not telling them, which they called a "lie of omission."

Ellen is trying to make problems go away by avoiding them. But instead of getting rid of one problem, she has created another on top of the first. When we don't face challenges head on, we make things worse.

try this

Tell what additional problem might arise because of these kids not facing their challenges head on.

Tracy felt so nervous around other kids that she would throw up in the girls' bathroom before school. But she wouldn't talk to the counselor her mom had found for her.

_____

_____

Rob scratched his dad's car door by running into it with his bike. He tried to cover up the scratch with dirt.

_____

_____

Amanda didn't understand the math homework, so she skipped math class on the day of the test.

_____

_____

Joe wasn't going to get home by curfew, and he knew his parents would be mad, so he stayed out all night to avoid them.

_____

_____

Michelle got bad headaches after her grandfather died. She didn't want to go to the doctor, so she didn't tell her mother.

_____

_____

now try this

Circle the phrases that describe things you have done, or seen other people do, to avoid facing challenges head on. Use the blank lines to add your own.

eat too much	drink alcohol	sleep too much
watch too much TV	work too much	avoid someone or something
lie	take drugs	isolate myself
stay home	overexercise	be overinvolved in activities
blame others	deny a problem	stay on the computer too long
run away	hurt myself	stop eating

_____

_____

Describe a challenge you are dealing with that feels difficult to face.

_____

_____

Tell what would happen if you avoided it by using one of the behaviors listed above.

_____

_____

Tell how your self-esteem would be affected if you did this.

_____

_____

Tell what would happen if you faced this challenge head on.

_____

_____

Tell how your self-esteem would be affected if you did this.

_____

_____

today's affirmation

Facing my challenges is the only way to solve them and
helps create healthy self-esteem.

the power of realistic goals

know this

Realistic goals have the greatest chance of being achieved. They often involve smaller, intermediate steps, called short-term goals. When you set realistic short-term goals, you have a better chance of achieving your long-term goals.

Having a thought is the first step toward creating what we want. We have learned that possibilities are limitless and that we are held back only by our own minds. So we know that we can dream big and have the power to make those dreams reality. However, we still need to take action. If we want to be a hairdresser, a parent, or a surgeon, we will not achieve those goals by lying on our bed dreaming about them.

Sometimes we have trouble achieving our goals because we set them too high. For example, we may think, *I'm going to turn my life around. This semester I'll join three clubs, learn to play an instrument, get a part-time job, and change my grades from Ds to straight As.* Or we may think, *I really want to get into better physical shape by running. I'm going to sign up for the marathon in two weeks.*

For most people, either of these goals would be unrealistic and cause too much physical and emotional pressure. Most of us would run out of energy and quit trying early on. We have a better chance of achieving bigger goals if we set them as long-term goals—something to accomplish over a longer period of time. Then we can set realistic short-term goals as steps toward our long-term goals. For example, the short-term goals of joining one club, deciding what instrument to play, applying for a job, and spending more time on homework and test preparation are realistic steps toward reaching the longer-term goal of turning our life around. The short-term goal of starting to run three times a week is a realistic step toward getting into better physical shape and someday running a marathon.

Knowing how to set realistic short- and long-term goals can help us create more successes and healthier self-esteem.

try this

A short-term goal is one to be achieved in the near future (such as passing tomorrow's test), whereas a long-term goal is one to be achieved in the more distant future (such as graduating from college.) Short- and long-term goals are relative to a person's age and situation.

For each of these statements, circle S if you think it would work best as a short-term goal and L if it would work best as a long-term goal.

S L speak Spanish fluently

S L watch a lacrosse match to see how it's played

S L fill out a job application

S L go to PE class

S L win a surfing competition

S L sign up for Spanish I

S L work as a camp counselor

S L go surfing for an hour each day

S L raise your PE grade

S L be the highest scorer on the lacrosse team

Write three to five short-term goals that would lead toward each of the following kids' long-term goals.

As a freshman, Becky hopes to sing a solo in the school chorus one day.

1. _____

2. _____

3. _____

4. _____

5. _____

Trevor wants to upgrade his phone but needs money to pay for it.

1. _____

2. _____

3. _____

4. _____

5. _____

Colin wants to get an article published in the school newspaper.

1. _____

2. _____

3. _____

4. _____

5. _____

Dyanna wants to go to the dance with Charles, but she has never actually met him.

1. _____

2. _____

3. _____

4. _____

5. _____

now try this

At the top of each ladder, write one long-term goal you would like to accomplish in the next six months. For each, write one short-term goal leading toward that on each rung of the ladder. Add more rungs if necessary.

My Long-Term Goal   *My Long-Term Goal*

_____   _____

Describe how you feel about yourself when you set your sights too high and then don't achieve your goal.

_____

_____

_____

Describe how you feel about yourself when you achieve a goal that you have wanted for a long time.

_____

_____

_____

today's affirmation

I think realistically to achieve my goals.

39 the power of support

know this

Human beings are created with limits. No one person can do everything. This reality forces us to interact with and help one another. Asking for help or support when you need it is a powerful tool for achieving your goals and maintaining healthy self-esteem.

Rachel and her mom were having a heavy disagreement. Rachel had been feeling really down. Her grades were dropping, and she was starting to isolate herself from her friends. Her mother said she should have someone outside the family to confide in and wanted her to talk to a counselor.

"I'm not going to tell my problems to some stranger who is paid to listen to me," said Rachel. "I'm fine. I just need to be left alone."

The next week Rachel's track coach pulled her aside after a meet and said her performance was declining drastically. Rachel admitted she was feeling bad and didn't know how to help herself. Nothing she tried seemed to work.

"I'd like to refer you to a therapist," her coach said, handing Rachel a business card. "Carolyn is a friend of mine and an awesome listener. She's worked with other girls on the team before. She went through a hard time in high school herself and knows how rough it can be. I'd like you to make an appointment with her—or I'm going to ask you to take a break from the track team."

Rachel realized she was losing things that were important to her. She told her mom about the therapist and made an appointment. The coach was right. Carolyn was kind and had firsthand experience with what Rachel was going through. She said Rachel's feelings were normal during adolescence; she just needed help handling them. Carolyn also had ideas for coping that Rachel hadn't thought of. Rachel admitted to Carolyn that she had been reluctant at first, but it did feel good to talk things out and get an objective opinion.

"That's normal, too," said Carolyn. "Sometimes we feel embarrassed or ashamed that we can't fix everything ourselves. But people are made to help each other. Otherwise we all would be able to repair our own cars, fill our own cavities, and coach our own sports teams. If people were supposed to be self-sufficient, we wouldn't need firefighters, lawyers, manicurists, or construction workers. We would all live completely independently and never have to interact.

"Asking for support when we need it is a sign of strength and wisdom. It means we are strong enough to face our problems instead of running away from them."

try this

Sometimes we may feel there is no one we could trust to help us even if we asked. We may know a lot of people but not believe we have any true friends. We may feel isolated or alone. But usually there is at least one person who believes in us, who would help us, and who would gladly be there if we reached out.

Write the name of one person who cares about you.

_____

Think of anyone else who believes in you, or whom you could turn to if you needed help. Who would stand up for you if someone was talking you down? Who would want to help if you were hurting? For each category, write the names of any other actual or possible support people in your life:

Family in my home:

_____

_____

Family outside of my home:

_____

_____

Friend:

_____

_____

Neighbor:

_____

_____

Counselor:

_____

_____

Coach:

_____

_____

Teacher:

_____

_____

Faith leader:

_____

_____

Pet:

_____

_____

Other:

_____

_____

Write in your name at the top of the pyramid. In the spaces below that, write the names of those who support you. Include anyone you listed above.

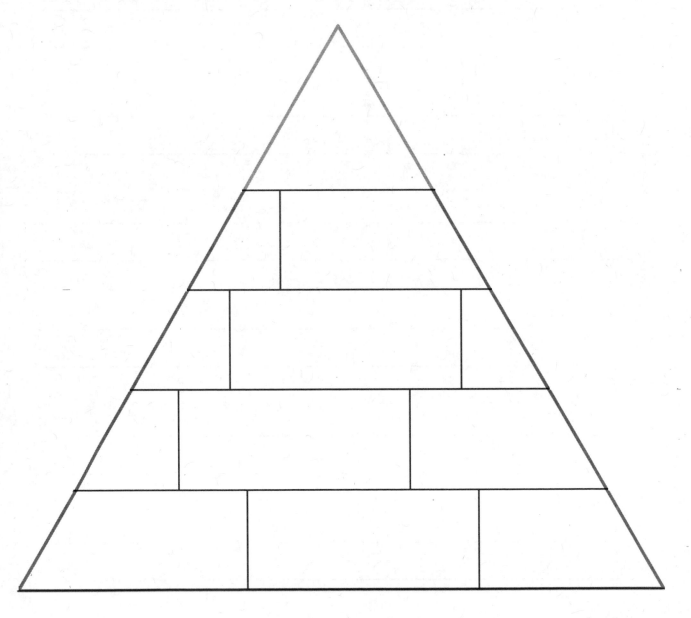

now try this

Write a letter to someone who cares about you and ask for that person's help. You don't actually have to send this letter, so say whatever is in your heart.

Describe how this person would support you if you reached out. What might he or she do or say to help?

_____

_____

Tell what it feels like to ask for help.

_____

_____

today's affirmation

Asking for help is an act of wisdom and healthy coping.

know this

Many people believe there is a power greater than themselves—that human beings did not create the universe, nor can they control it. If you believe in a power greater than yourself, you can tap that power to help you meet the challenges of life.

Human beings are amazing creatures. Through our ability to think and create, we have transformed our world by discovering ways to fly without wings, communicate by transmitting voices and images through space, bring heat and light into our homes even when our environment is cold and dark, repair our physical forms with bone replacements and organ transplants, and set foot on the moon.

We govern nations, educate our citizens, travel underwater, build skyscrapers, and program computers. We discover cures for disease and invent machines to wash our clothes, slice our bread, and take pictures of our brains. We express our gifts through art, literature, and music.

And yet, despite all our incredible skills, talents, and accomplishments, we did not set the planets into orbit or create more than 20,000 species of fish and 900,000 types of insects. We did not design the system whereby water evaporates from lakes and oceans so it can rain down to sustain life on land. We did not invent the method whereby two microscopic cells combine to grow into a new human being during a nine-month stay in a womb.

When we comprehend that something greater than ourselves is at work in the universe, continually creating and sustaining the magnificent and complex diversity of miracles in our world, we can use our understanding of and our relationship to that higher power to help us through life.

try this

Circle any of the words below that help describe your understanding of a power greater than yourself.

life force	nature	god	peace	spirit
love	divinity	holiness	hope	meaning
faith	energy	eternity	gratitude	miracles
wisdom	purpose	heart	heaven	prayer
natural law	flow	joy	universe	infinite

Check any of the statements below that are similar to your own beliefs.

☐ There is a reason for everything.

☐ I am loved.

☐ There is a plan for my life.

☐ I can trust in a higher power.

☐ Everything works out for the best.

☐ There is a power greater than myself.

☐ Prayer and thought can create change.

☐ I can be guided by a higher power.

☐ I am part of the divine flow of life.

☐ God doesn't make garbage, so I am a valuable piece of the universe.

Add any additional statements that reflect your beliefs.

_____

_____

_____

Draw a symbol, or use line, color, or form to describe your belief about a higher power.

now try this

If the flow of the universe is kept in motion by a higher power, describe how you are more in sync with that flow when you are accepting of yourself. How are you less in sync with that flow when you express self-hatred and harshness toward yourself?

_____

_____

_____

Tell if you think having healthy self-esteem contributes positively or negatively to the rest of the universe.

_____

_____

_____

Tell how a belief in a higher power might help you in the following situations:

You learn that your date went out with someone else after canceling on you.

_____

_____

_____

You don't like your body.

_____

_____

_____

You stutter when giving your oral presentation.

_____

_____

_____

You turn in five different job applications, and none of the employers call you back.

_____

_____

_____

Read the following prayer that people often use to find peace within themselves:

Grant me the serenity to accept the things I cannot change,

The courage to change the things I can,

And the wisdom to know the difference.

If those words feel good to you, use them to help you find your own peace. If they do not work for you, write your own prayer or hope, using words that help you connect to the peace of your personal higher power.

_____

_____

_____

today's affirmation

A higher power can help and support me.

Lisa M. Schab, LCSW, is a licensed clinical social worker with a private counseling practice in the greater Chicago area. She has authored fourteen selfhelp books and workbooks for children, teens, and adults, including The Anxiety Workbook for Teens and Beyond the Blues. Schab teaches selfhelp workshops for the general public and training seminars for professionals, and is a member of the National Association of Social Workers (NASW) and the National Association of Anorexia Nervosa and Associated Disorders (ANAD).